runes

talk to the
woman within

runes

talk to the
woman within

teach yourself to rely on her support

cassandra eason

quantum

LONDON • NEW YORK • TORONTO • SYDNEY

quantum

An imprint of W. Foulsham & Co. Ltd
The Publishing House, Bennetts Close,
Cippenham, Slough, Berkshire, SL1 5AP, England

ISBN 0–572–02612-9

Copyright © 2000 Cassandra Eason

All rights reserved.

The Copyright Act prohibits (subject to certain very
limited exceptions) the making of copies of any copyright work
or of a substantial part of such a work, including the making of
copies by photocopying or similar process. Written permission
to make a copy or copies must therefore normally be obtained from
the publisher in advance. It is advisable also to consult the
publisher if in any doubt as to the legality of any copying
which is to be undertaken.

Printed in Great Britain by St. Edmundsbury Press, Bury St. Edmunds, Suffolk.

Contents

Introduction

Runes follow a strong female tradition. In the thirteenth century, the author of the Viking saga of Erik the Red described a rune mistress:

She wore a cloak set with stones along the hem. Around her neck and covering her head she wore a hood lined with white catskins. In one hand she carried a staff with a knob on the end and from her belt, holding together her long dress, hung a charm pouch.

Runic divination was practised formally by wise women while warriors were away at war or searching for new lands for conquest and trade. Men would cast the runes before a battle or a voyage to learn the will of the gods with the cast of the cup.

The Vikings were great voyagers – Leif, son of Erik the Red, discovered America in 992, 500 years before Columbus – and they travelled to Russia, Turkey, Greece and North Africa. Along their routes can be found stone monuments, graves and artefacts marked with runes.

Runic rituals and divination were carried out not only by the female shaman of the clan, but also by ordinary women at night by the fire in their homesteads, to see whether their husbands and sons would return and whether the family would survive the harshness of a Northern winter. As they cast the magical runes, wives, sisters and mothers endowed them with hopes, fears, dreams and desires.

In our world of central heating and artificial light, the physical perils may have diminished, but we share the same concerns for ourselves and our loved ones and the need to find our true selves, as did those strong women of the world of ice and snow.

What are runes?

Rune means secret or hidden and derives from *ru*, the word for whisper in the ancient Teutonic languages. Runes are consistent, distinctive, angular symbols, marked on round stones, wooden discs or wooden staves, to form a set of anything from 16 to 36 runes, depending on the particular region in which they were used.

Runes were used in the Scandinavian world as far north as Iceland, among the Anglo-Saxons on the plains of western Europe and in those lands the Germanic peoples conquered, including Northumberland in the north-east of England where an extended runic system developed, that drew on the ancient concepts of Earth, Air, Fire and Water.

These symbols can be used for divination, magic or meditation, and when runic forms are combined as Bind Runes they create a magical talisman of power or protection. Each runic symbol corresponds approximately to a letter and runes sometimes form a magical alphabet for encoding and thereby empowering magical wishes.

The legend of Odin, the Viking All-father, who invented the runes, probably comes from an ancient tribe known as the Volsungr who originated from the Far North during the last Ice Age. They were a tribe of priest–magicians who were said to guard the ancient forests and trackways, helping any in need and using an early form of runes known as the Ur Runes. The Volsungr spread their wisdom, including the sacred incantations associated with the magical symbols, but eventually disappeared back into the Northern forests. These early runic symbols, many of them sacred signs from the Bronze Age associated with the Mother Goddess, are found in great quantity in ancient rock carvings in Sweden, dating from 1300–1200 BC, during the second Bronze Age, and from 800–600 BC, the transition period from the Iron Age.

The runic systems that remain in use today date from the second or third centuries BC when the Germanic peoples came in touch through increasing trade links across Europe as far as the Baltic with the Mediterranean Etruscan alphabet system.

How are runes of relevance today?

The runic system is based on archetypes and concepts that underpin all divination systems, and parallels can be found with both Tarot and crystals. Runes talk of birth, death, relationships and money and finding meaning in a changing and sometimes hostile world.

The runic world is one that recognises and respects the natural world of trees, storms, rain, hail and snow as well as sunshine, plains, the sea and mountains. But above all it has a very modern view of fate: that our future is made up of our past and present. Some modern psychologists even agree with the Viking view that we carry the burdens of our ancestors in our genes. For in a sense what we are is created not only from our immediate families, but their most distant forebears in a complex web of interconnections.

The Vikings perceived fate as a web constantly being woven and rewoven. The three Norns, or Fates, of the Northern world are not the creatures of blind fortune, but are women who weave the web on our behalf. We cannot protect ourselves against misfortune, any more than the ancient peoples of the runic were proof against the dangers of their world. But if we absorb the wisdom of the runes through them, we can take control of our destiny.

Women are remarkably free of illusion. We may crave romance and indulge in passion but we understand better than most men the consequences of action and see beyond the surface of relationships, accepting fallibility in others and the need to rebuild rather than cast away (the Norns were, after all, women).

We may be as thrusting as the Viking or Anglo-Saxon warriors in a project that matters to us, but have wider vision so that we can feed the children, comfort sick or unhappy friends or family and expand the time to match the need – not the other way round. It is no accident that the powerful Mother Goddess Frigga (or Frigg or Frige, as she is known in the Anglo-Saxon tradition) was also patron of women, marriage and housewives. Her shining distaff may be seen in the stars, in the constellation we now call Orion's Belt. And unlike her husband Odin (or Woden in the Anglo-Saxon tradition) she did not go off wandering for months on end each year, allowing winter to come in his absence and ravage the land.

How can we use the runes?

This book introduces a simple but potent system of casting the runes, based on a circle cloth and using multiples of three runes. Though the casting, or throwing, of the runes would seem apparently random, I have found that the runes selected build up a relevant picture of predominant issues, hidden factors and potential solutions.

Time and again over hundreds of readings I have witnessed runes being cast in specific formations that answer questions even deeper than the original one posed. Divination seems to operate by a method akin to psychokinesis, whereby the runes our hand selects unseen from within the rune bag and the way they fall on the cloth are influenced by our deep unconscious wisdom. The psychologist Carl Gustav Jung believed this was linked with the collective wisdom of all mankind in all times and places and operated beyond the constraints of time and space.

The original rune casts invoked the power of the gods and goddesses. In the modern world, many of us identify more readily with the divus, or deity within, our own evolved spiritual self. Its power is the same one we use in the everyday world to assess whether a stranger is trustworthy or not, a decision that may go counter to external appearances or the available evidence. Invariably these instinctive judgements are correct. Mothers often wake in the night before their child does and correctly predict the sex of an unborn child without, or even contrary to, the evidence of a scan. Women tend to trust the inner voice more than men do and so can more readily access the hidden part of the mind that finds expression through the runes.

The wisdom of the runes

Much of the current rune lore springs from a series of rune poems based on poems and stories handed down by word of mouth that were recorded from about the eleventh century onwards in Scandinavia and from the ninth century or even earlier in Northern Europe (the originals have been lost, which makes dating of the old legends difficult). The poems were written down by monks, and the copies reflect the Christian viewpoint of the scribes but still capture much of the early dangers and hardships of the pioneers and warriors who first adopted the runes as a guide. The three main poems are the Anglo-Saxon (or Old English) rune poem, the Old Norse rune poem and the Icelandic rune poem.

There are many versions of Odin the Viking All-father's account of the discovery of runes and their inherent wisdom, suggesting that runes contained knowledge and wisdom beyond even that possessed by the deities. This knowledge was seen as stemming from the depths of time, from the roots of Yggdrassil, the Norse World Tree, in the Anglo-Saxon tradition called Eormensyll, in which were set the nine worlds, including those inhabited by gods and mortals. The three Norns, or Goddesses of Destiny, were believed to guard the Well of Urd (or Wyrd or Fate) at the foot of the first root of Yggdrassil, directly below the realm of the gods, Asgard.

The following is an account, said to be dictated by Odin himself, of his self-inflicted ordeal to find runic enlightenment:

> *Wounded I hung on Yggdrassil*
> *For nine nights long*
> *Pierced by a spear*
> *Consecrated to Odin,*
> *… sacrifice to myself*
> *Upon that tree*
> *The wisest know not the roots*
> *of ancient times whence it sprang.*
> *None brought me bread*
> *None gave me mead*
> *Down to the depths I searched*
> *I took up the Runes …*
> *And from that Tree I fell*
> *Screaming.*

(From the *Sayings of the High One* from the *Elder Edda*, an adaptation of several translations of early Icelandic legends and poems.)

Variations in the legends are mainly in the form of different names for the deities and their importance; for example, Thunor, the Anglo-Saxon god of thunder, the equivalent of the Norse Thor, is of greater importance in the Anglo-Saxon than the Viking cosmology. The runes also have slightly different names in the different systems, though similar meanings.

Should you read the runes for yourself or other people?

Though it is traditionally said that you should not read the runes for yourself, they are a powerful tool of self-discovery and are a means of developing spiritual awareness as well as answering questions concerning the everyday world. Of course, you can read runes for others, but any divinatory reading is essentially a dialogue with the questioner.

The runes and women

Never have there been more opportunities for women, or more pressures. We no longer simply watch the longboat sailing away – women now serve at sea themselves, as well as taking active roles in the other armed forces, fly the world as pilots and even explore space.

But open any women's magazine and it is full of articles on how to get and keep your man, perform sexual gymnastics and fight off cellulite, while the home sections generally depict a woman whipping up a delicious meal, having slipped off her power suit to clean the bathroom with a new wonder gel, before redecorating the lounge and rearranging the furniture to get the feng shui flowing.

Having a family is a great joy, but even in lands where paternity leave is statutory, women in practice still, according to surveys, do most of the child care and household chores. An older woman may find herself responsible for the care of her mother or even grandmother, while even a woman without dependants has the worries of redundancy and ageing in a society that worships youth.

Women's lives used to be guided by the Moon and at menstruation they would retire to the Moon Lodge on the Dark of the Moon to rest and contemplate. But we have become a 24-hour, 365-day society, no longer resting during the long nights of winter in preparation for the spring. Women especially suffer, working almost until they go into labour, opening windows wide at high-powered meetings to offset hot flushes, accepting HRT even if they do not want it, in their efforts to keep up with the frenetic pace of living rather than slowing down and allowing nature to carry them to the next stage. Even the young and glamorous are not immune from the pressures. Recent surveys have indicated that a high proportion of younger women would sooner read or go to sleep than indulge in sex.

But all is not doom and gloom, for women can cope with a dozen demands on their time and have rich relationships as well as developing their careers. The connection is still there with the Moon and the natural world and women can, through such divinatory and magical devices as the runes, connect with their spiritual natures and can use inspiration and intuition to resolve issues in the everyday world that defy logic and expert opinion. Through rune rituals they can empower themselves, gain protection from the hostility of others and above all understand the purpose of their lives and shape their destiny, spiritually, emotionally and practically.

Finding your runes

Unlike many divinatory tools, runes are very easy to make and because you have not only selected the stones but drawn the magical symbols on each one, they become a part of your own special magic.

You need 30 flat pebbles, each about the size of a large coin. Each should have a suitable surface on one side on which to draw or engrave the symbol.

If at all possible, collect your rune pebbles on a day spent by the sea or on the shore of a lake or tidal river. I once read a poem by e.e. cummings in which he explained:

> *Whatever you lose like a you or a me, it's always yourself*
> *you find by the sea.*

That seems to mirror the purpose of finding your own runes. But you can use any stones you find, whether in a desert or an urban park, as each will carry the energies of the land.

Wherever you look, you should make the occasion a happy one, filled with tranquillity, so it is not advisable to hunt for runes with anyone who will demand your attention. Take your time and let the stones choose you. Wash them in the sea or river if you are close to one and watch how even the most matt stones then sparkle like jewels. Let them speak to your inner ear and close your eyes as you hold each one.

If you are by the sea, walk on the beach and write your name in the sand as you did when you were a child. Only your name – no one else's. Now outline it with your runes before putting them away. If you are in a park, mark your initials in runes on a flat area of grass in a quiet spot.

Collect your blank runes one by one and place them in a drawstring bag, if possible made of a natural fabric.

Alternatively, go to a forest and find a dry branch that you can cut to make 30 discs of approximately the same size (a broom handle works just as well, but if you have the opportunity, walk among the trees – you may hear them speak as did the priestesses in the ancient oak groves of Dodona, that were sacred to Zeus). The oak, the tree of Thor and Odin, is a good choice, as is ash, the Teutonic World Tree. Hazel was the Druidic tree of wisdom and justice and is another good choice for divination, but you can make runes with any wood.

You can, if you are gifted, create silver runes, ceramic ones or paint your symbols on 30 clear crystals of rose quartz or pale transparent amethyst.

You may decide to buy a rune set, in which case, for the purposes of this book, ask for an Anglo-Saxon set which will have 29 runes plus a blank. There are beautiful sets made of crystals, silver and stone as well as wood. Take your time and choose the one that feels right for you.

Find a place, however small, in your home or garden if possible that you can use for your magical work. You can adapt a table or cupboard to keep candles, crystals, your rune cloth and your bag of runes, perhaps in a special wooden box when not in use. As you work here quietly over the coming weeks, the harmonious energies will accumulate so that it becomes a sanctuary in the busiest home. Keep fresh flowers or plants in your special place to increase the flow of the Life Force.

In the evening, light candles of purple and deep blue for psychic awareness, and burn an incense such as a jasmine, fragrance of the Moon, or sandalwood for wisdom, and connect with your own spiritual nature. Spread your own blank runes or the set you purchased before you. They represent the destiny that you will write for yourself and so they are very special.

✣ On this first evening, around your runes sprinkle a circle of salt to give them the protection of the ancient Earth element, saying:

> *Mother Earth, let my runes reflect the wise ways of the ancestors to accept what cannot be changed.*

✢ Next, make next a clockwise circle of smoke from your jasmine or sandalwood incense, saying:

> *Power of Earth, let my runes speak true and cut through illusion and inertia.*

✢ Now, make a circle of fire, using the candle flame, saying:

> *Power of fire, let my runes soar so that they can uncover possibilities as yet undreamed-of.*

✢ Finally, sprinkle rainwater that has not touched the ground before collection on top of the circle of salt, saying:

> *Power of Water, may my runes bring healing and reconciliation to all who cast them.*

You have now created a triple circle of power and protection around your runes. Leave the runes in the circle until the candles have burned down and then place them carefully in your rune bag and sleep with them next to your bed. You may dream of all those possibilities as yet unwritten.

The runes

The rune set we have illustrated is based on the Northumbrian runes, a later version of the Anglo-Saxon runes. If you buy an Anglo-Saxon set, Yr will have the symbol ᚻ, but this is the only real difference. The Northumbrian set has four additional runes, influenced by Celtic Christianity, but these are not used in this book.

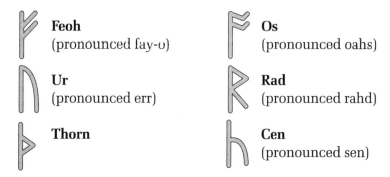

Feoh
(pronounced fay-o)

Os
(pronounced oahs)

Ur
(pronounced err)

Rad
(pronounced rahd)

Thorn

Cen
(pronounced sen)

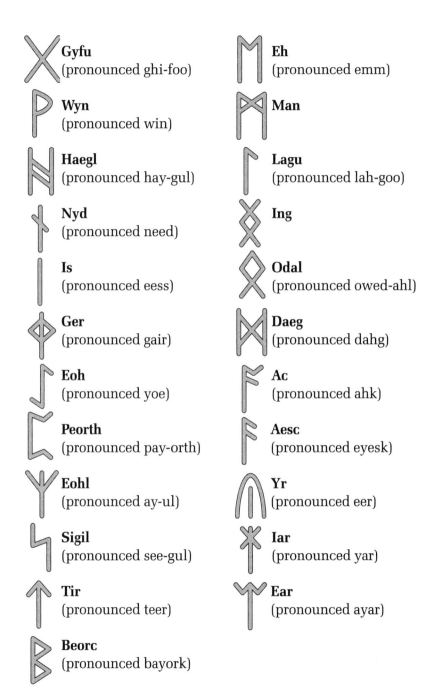

Gyfu
(pronounced ghi-foo)

Wyn
(pronounced win)

Haegl
(pronounced hay-gul)

Nyd
(pronounced need)

Is
(pronounced eess)

Ger
(pronounced gair)

Eoh
(pronounced yoe)

Peorth
(pronounced pay-orth)

Eohl
(pronounced ay-ul)

Sigil
(pronounced see-gul)

Tir
(pronounced teer)

Beorc
(pronounced bayork)

Eh
(pronounced emm)

Man

Lagu
(pronounced lah-goo)

Ing

Odal
(pronounced owed-ahl)

Daeg
(pronounced dahg)

Ac
(pronounced ahk)

Aesc
(pronounced eyesk)

Yr
(pronounced eer)

Iar
(pronounced yar)

Ear
(pronounced ayar)

Marking your runes

You can either engrave all your runes together or make one each evening or morning and learn its significance, creating your system rune by rune. The latter method allows the system to evolve naturally. If you have bought a set of runes, miss out this section and spend the time holding each rune in turn and writing or drawing any impressions it creates. You may be surprised how close you are to the actual meanings for the runes.

✢ Close your eyes and pull a pebble or piece of wood at random from your bag and mark it. On stone use either a red or black permanent marker or paint. Red was the traditional colour for rune markings, but many people find black clearer.

✢ If you are using wood, etch the shape into the wood with an awl or screwdriver and then paint the symbol on the indentation. Alternatively, you can burn in the shape, carefully using a red-hot screwdriver or a pyrographic tool, which can be bought from an art or hobby shop.

✢ If this is your first rune set, you may wish to create a simple temporary set using stones and a marker – the magic is within you, not the runes. Later you can buy or create a special set when you are familiar with rune-casting and know what is right for you.

✢ Practise drawing each symbol on paper so that you can create it with easy, confident movements. Visualise it carved in golden light or fire on your rune.

✢ You may wish to read about each rune before you create it. If you do, then spend a little time thinking abut each rune and what it symbolises. You might even like to recite a mantra about the rune as you create it. For example, Feoh, the first rune, is connected with prosperity. Therefore your chant might be:

Feoh, feoh, bring me abundance.

✢ If possible, do something to make yourself happy each evening before creating your rune, or spend a few minutes in quiet contemplation of the rune meaning, so that you associate each rune with positive feelings.

✢ If you are very busy or feel negative, leave your rune-making until another day and instead perhaps spend a few minutes sitting quietly, gazing into a candle flame, before you go to sleep, or burn rose, geranium or lavender oil to restore your inner harmony.

✢ Equally, you may have a free day when you want to work on your runes, so adapt the methods I have outlined to fit with your own needs, taking as many or as few days as you need to learn the system.

Getting to know your runes

Over the next few chapters, I have given the traditional meaning for each rune, and then outlined areas of life to which it refers. Although you have already consecrated your blank runes, you may wish to empower each individual rune as you meet it for the first time, whether it is one you have made or one you have bought. You can do this by sprinkling a few grains of sea salt on it and passing it through a red candle while repeating your mantra of power that encapsulates the meaning of the rune.

Each evening after you have made or read about the rune, sit in the candlelight holding it between your hands and let images or words flow through your mind, linking each symbol with your life.

You may wish afterwards to note some of these initial associations in your journal, and as you work with the runes you will gain new impressions. If this seems difficult, tell the story for the rune, beginning with the images I have reproduced from the ancient rune poems. If you wish, place the rune beneath your pillow and you may dream of the world of ice and snow.

When you have three or four runes, you can pick one from the bag and see what it says about your life and continue the individual rune story. Since each of the runes is relevant on a spiritual as well as mental and material level, these moments of quiet contemplation can help to make the rune set uniquely your own.

The blank side of the rune

Each of your runes will have one blank side, but this is not like the reverse of a playing or Tarot card. The blank can tell you as much about yourself and the reading as the marked side of the rune. When your rune does fall on the cloth blank-side uppermost, turn it over and examine the issue, whether for yourself or a questioner, very gently. Sometimes unresolved matters will emerge spontaneously as you evolve spiritually and be reflected in these blank aspects cast in a reading.

If you can discover what it is that holds you back from the action or decision reflected in the symbol on the marked face, you can decide whether you wish to wait or to withdraw from a situation, albeit temporarily. However, the blank side of the rune may prompt you to a conscious decision to confront and overcome mental or spiritual blocks. Sometimes doubts or fears may be valid or the time is not right, especially if a particular rune is one that frequently appears in your readings with the marked side uppermost. The other runes in the reading will usually clarify this for you but, if in doubt, hold the rune in your cupped hands and close your eyes, letting impressions form; they may be visual, in words or just general feelings.

Keeping a runic diary

When you begin your rune work, you may find it helpful to record the rune you select each day in a notebook or diary. Over the subsequent days, you will see a pattern emerging. Note your readings over a period of weeks. It is surprising how quickly you can forget the details of even a significant rune cast.

You can also record readings you do for others and collect together your own meanings for particular runes, any rituals you devise and lists of useful herbs, oils, incenses and crystals. As with any other journal, you can watch your life unfold and as you look back over what you have written, you will realise how far you have travelled spiritually. A loose-leaf folder is useful, as you can add pages and revise interpretations, and you may like to have a special leather or velvet journal in which you record events in your life that had earlier been augured in the runes.

Rune rows

Runes are divided into aetts or sets of eight runes. Each rune row was ruled by a particular deity or common theme: the aett of Freyja, the aett of Haegl, the aett of Tir and the aett of Odin.

DAY 1
Feoh – wealth

Prosperity, financial affairs, the price that must be paid

Feoh is the first rune in the aett of Freyja, the goddess of love, beauty and fertility. The basic meaning of Feoh is wealth in the sense of money or currency of any sort. Cattle were mobile currency, a measurement of one's wealth in the Viking world. Our word 'fee' comes from this term and so the rune has the added meaning of the price one must pay for any action – or inaction. Indeed, the old Norse and Icelandic rune poems warn that money causes strife among kinsmen, although the Old English or Anglo-Saxon rune poem talks of the joys of material comfort, as long as money is used wisely and shared freely with others.

Feoh in a reading

The rune may have a straightforward meaning, indicating that you are planning a new money-making venture that augurs success. Or you may need to reorganise your finances so that you are more in control. But Feoh may also refer to the price you are paying, or need to pay, either to maintain the status quo or to initiate change. This price may manifest not only in material terms, but also in terms of peace of mind and the freedom to be what you are deep inside.

So the future may involve perhaps risking financial security for a new venture that will bring great fulfilment emotionally or spiritually. Conversely, you may need to work single-mindedly for a while to achieve success in financial terms so that you can travel, buy a home or provide security for your dependants. Most women are aware that you cannot evolve spiritually very easily if you are constantly worried about paying the bills. Gurus who scorn the material world all too often turn out to have a penthouse in Manhattan and a ranch in Arizona. The key to Feoh is choosing your path and accepting the price that you must pay.

Hidden Feoh

When the blank face of Feoh is uppermost in a reading, there may be unresolved resentment in the area of money. For money is an emotive issue in all kinds of relationships: even quite liberated men can feel threatened if their partners are higher earners than they are. Or perhaps you are sharing expenses with a flatmate or family, and this is causing friction. Mothers can sometimes feel they are little more than a talking cash machine to offspring, especially adult ones who may remain in the nest until their mid-twenties or even thirties and use their own money for partying and exotic holidays. Whatever the scenario, it is important to resolve the problem before it causes a major rift – and that may mean asserting your rights.

There may also be hidden factors that are keeping you in a situation from which you believe you wish to escape. Sometimes there is an underlying advantage in a situation that to others may seem unsatisfactory. Women who subsidise adult children (and I include myself here) are afraid of no longer being needed if they cut the financial umbilical cord. A woman who works for less-than-satisfactory employers may stay because she feels deep down that she is central to the smooth running or harmony of the office; she is being compensated on an emotional level for the material or practical shortcomings of her workplace.

Examine those areas of your life where you are constantly striving for change but failing: ask yourself if you really want change. If not, that is a positive decision in itself. Above all, we must value ourselves and be sure of our priorities.

DAY 2
Ur – the auroch

Overcoming obstacles, survival instincts and courage

The auroch was a huge, wild, very fierce ox, much like the Longhorn cattle of modern times. The horns of these creatures were worn on Viking helmets, engraved with the Ur rune to transfer the strength of the auroch to warriors by associative magic. The last aurochs still roamed the plains of Northern Europe in 1627.

The Norse and Icelandic rune poems speak about hardship for the herdsmen and purification through suffering, using the images of iron and of obstacles to be overcome by strength and endurance. In the Anglo-Saxon rune poem, the auroch is described as courageous, fearless, knowing no limits.

So this is not the rune of the delicate maiden waiting for her knight in shining armour to fight off the dragon, but one of the warrior venturing forth boldly, brandishing a bloody axe.

Ur in a reading

Ur speaks of primal strength and the courage to grasp what we want and overcome any obstacles in our way. We may meet few charging herds of aurochs in the modern world, but we all need strength and determination to stand firm at some times, and so when you cast Ur there may be a need to overcome opposition or to fight for what you want.

Although most women are naturally strong in any crisis and will face any hardship or danger to protect those they love, the concept of strong women still strikes fear in the heart of men who are uncertain about their own masculinity; ironically, these are often the most macho of guys on the surface. But this is the rune of supreme effort and if you have a burning desire to achieve a dream and you are prepared to give your all, Ur promises you will succeed.

You may have to be strong in a situation where others are hesitating: perhaps you have a family crisis, or you have to stand against someone at work who is trying to bully you or force through changes you know are wrong. Or perhaps you may need to show tough love with those close to your heart, to coerce a partner, child or friend to try again after a setback: you may even have to go out there yourself, ignoring your fears and pushing away your exhaustion.

Hidden Ur

This represents the obstructive aspect of the rune. Ask yourself if you really do want to make that trip, move house, have published the novel that gave you such pleasure to write, propose to the guy of your dreams, or get divorced – there are hints here of hidden Feoh with which hidden Ur often appears. Many times we tell ourselves we will join an aerobics class or a computer course or apply for promotion, but it is always next week, when Christmas is over, when the children are older, or the weather is better, when we have redecorated the house. We cannot take our Advanced Driving Test, trek to Tibet or keep Sundays for ourselves because of work rotas, or because we always meet a certain friend for lunch, or we have to visit a relative or play tennis. My own list of 'one day I will' extends into the twenty-second century. Sometimes, however, there are real obstacles – and that is where Ur in its positive aspect comes into play.

It may be that we unconsciously impose obstacle after obstacle in the path of change because deep down we are too frightened of failure, or do not really want to change jobs or move home but are being pressurised by the expectations of others. It is a question of honest assessment. If you are afraid of what others will say or of rejection, summon the courage of Ur to initiate change. However, if you are happy with your life, do not feel you have to reach some standard of perfection that is at odds with your own world view. If you have no burning desire for lifestyle changes, enjoy your life as it is. You already have what many seek: true contentment.

DAY 3
Thorn – the hammer of Thor

Protection, challenges, secrecy and conflicts

Thorn is associated with another harsh image, the thorn trees, although thorns can have a protective role against intruders. Bramble or hawthorn bushes have been used to hedge boundaries since ancient times and were traditionally grown in many parts of Europe around the homes of those who practised magic, so giving Thorn the subsidiary meaning of secrecy.

In pre-Christian times, the sign of the hammer was a sacred mark of protection and the thorn rune was drawn, or signed, to call upon other similar powers. In the Norse and Icelandic poems, Thorn is associated with the Thurs, a legendary giant, and Thuriasz is the Norse name for this rune. There were several groups of rime-thurses, or Frost Giants, who fought with the gods, so Thorn is a rune of challenge to those who seek to make changes or go against outmoded tradition.

The Anglo-Saxon rune poem is perhaps the clearest indicator of the way the thorn is regarded, telling of how it is cruel to anyone who lies on it and sharp to the grasp. But it does offer protection to the vulnerable flower or fruit on a tree or bush.

Thorn is also associated with Thor, god of thunder and courage, who sought to protect Asgard, realm of the gods, from the Frost Giants. Thor had a magic hammer, Mjöllnir, that always returned to his hand after it had reached its target. As well as defending the gods against the Frost Giants, Thor's hammer acted as a sacred symbol at marriages, births and funerals. The tradition of eloping and marrying at the forge in Gretna Green in Scotland recalls this ancient symbolism.

Thorn in a reading

The challenging aspect of Thorn is to the fore, but in the most positive way. You may need to challenge the status quo at work or to confront someone close to you about behaviour that is hurtful or destructive. If you are a natural peace-maker, you may find it difficult to take a stand over an injustice, especially if other people are urging you – perhaps through their own self-interest – not to make a fuss.

The secrecy aspect may come to the fore if you are challenging officialdom, recalcitrant teenagers or a partner or lover who is being less than open with you. It may be that the other person does not want to worry you, but usually any situation is better brought out in the open where it can be resolved, perhaps by using some of that Ur primal strength. Therefore you may need to penetrate a hedge of self-interest, so be careful to protect yourself while wielding the hammer of Thor that always strikes true.

On the other hand, you may need to protect those you love and your mother-wolf side may come to the fore, perhaps to protect a vulnerable colleague, child or partner who is under attack; sometimes just by being there you can offer immeasurable support.

Hidden Thorn

However successful we may be in public, we all have a vulnerable core and it is easy to be hurt by the barbs of others. Often it is not major issues but the small wounds and injustices that can build up the thorns out of all proportion. Women absorb the spite and anger of others and sometimes eat, drink or smoke too much as a way of literally swallowing resentment; but the stress may cause them to develop migraines, neck pains or allergies.

It is therefore vital to protect yourself from negativity by turning the barb outwards towards the perpetrator of the selfishness or malice, not to wound them but to shield yourself. 'No' and 'I do mind' are words that women sometimes find hard to say to friends, family or unthinking colleagues, whether the request is one for babysitting when you have planned a weekend away or consistently working late while others leave for home. Perhaps you may be the victim of some gossip, or criticism 'for your own good' from someone who perhaps resents your success or happiness or masks their own insecurity by projecting personal faults on to you. Whatever the cause, it hurts – but you do not have to bear it in silence.

DAY 4
Os – the mouth of Odin

Inspiration, wisdom, ideals and communication

This is the Father Rune, the rune of Odin, the All-father. Odin was desperate to acquire the wisdom and knowledge of the older order of giants. Having traded one of his eyes for wisdom and obtained the knowledge of the runes by sacrificing himself on the World Tree, he then obtained the gift of divine utterance. But some of the gift fell to earth and inspired mortal poetry, and from time to time Odin would favour mortals or one of the deities and share a little of the poetic mead.

The Norse rune poem talks of the 'estuary as the way of most journeys' conveying the concept that communication is essential for transforming inspiration into reality. In the Anglo-Saxon poem, the mouth is said to be the origin of every speech and the mainstay of wisdom, a warning indeed that we should consider the effect of our words before speaking.

Os in a reading

You have something important to communicate whether verbally or in writing. You can express your needs and feelings, confident that this is a good time to receive a positive response. Dialogue and persuasion are the way forward, rather than independent action or coercion. As the rune is associated with ideals and principles, the issue under discussion may be a core one and so this may be a time for exploring every aspect of a future plan, especially if it involves others, to avoid misunderstandings later.

Because Odin was the god of the muse, it may be a good time for advancing a literary, artistic or dramatic venture, whether for pleasure or professionally.

Os is the rune of wisdom and you may need to seek wise advice, either by consulting a traditional source, such as books, or by expressing your feelings and thoughts to someone who is an expert in the field in question.

Above all, Os is the rune of inspiration, so you will be entering an especially inspired period of your life when you have boundless energy and original ideas by the score. It is a good time for developing spiritually and you may find that your psychic progress may be spontaneous, rapid and rewarding.

Hidden Os

You may not be communicating your real needs and feelings but may be locked in an old dialogue within your head, unresolved in the past, perhaps even left from childhood. It is all too easy not to hear what is actually being said but rather to anticipate rejection or criticism, listening to a re-run of voices from the past. Maybe we are hearing the words of a parent disappointed with his or her own life, a teacher who found children a threat, a spiteful ex-lover or partner, jealous colleagues from a time when we were too young to see that the problem did not lie in our own shortcomings but in those who needed to diminish our self-esteem. Because many women are so sensitive and in tune with the reactions of others, even relatively small past rejections can leave lasting wounds and prevent clear communication of present needs and feelings.

DAY 5
Rad – the wheel

Travel, change, action, cycles of life, initiative and impetus

This symbol was portrayed in the pre-runic system as the sun wheel, which turned in the skies through its cycles of day and night and the solar year. Rad also represents the wheel on the wagon of the old fertility gods, as they gave new life to the fields (see also the rune Ing). Equally, Rad is associated with the constellations of stars around the cosmic axis.

Rad is, according to the Norse rune poem, the rune of the long and dangerous ride, 'the worst for horses'. The poem also refers to the best sword forged by Regin, the wise dwarf. For the young hero Sigurd, Regin made a sword from the pieces of his late father Sigmund's sword, a weapon so powerful that it could not be broken. Thus armed, Sigurd rode to avenge his father's death. Action and sometimes uncertainty are inevitable if we are to ride forward into life, but it is important to be like Sigurd, well prepared. The Anglo-Saxon rune poem contrasts the ease of the ancient warriors in their halls, talking about old victories and battles, while the snow falls outside.

Rad in a reading

Rad says it is time for action and change, time to put into practice all your plans and preparations. The time may not seem ideal – after all this is a rune of snow and hail outside – but we cannot always wait for perfect circumstances. Perhaps your action may involve an actual journey or taking the initiative to bring fresh impetus into your life. This is a very exciting rune and the new ideas may be bubbling inside you, offering new directions in either your personal or work life.

There may be opposition to your plans for change, especially from those close to you. When a man says to a woman he loves, 'Don't ever change', he may be voicing his own insecurity. An older women can find it very restricting when a partner retires and expects her to settle down to garden and fireside at a time when she is free from her own responsibilities, perhaps for the first time in years, and wants to explore the world, open a shop or go to university. Children, too, can be remarkably conservative when a mother or grandmother makes plans that do not include them.

The incentives to stay in that warm hall telling old stories may be great, but whether you are fleeing the parental nest for the first time, leaving a restrictive relationship, or simply developing new directions within a happy one, the first steps may be daunting. But once the change is set in motion, the impetus builds up and before long you are moving effortlessly along your new path.

Hidden Rad

This rune asks the question, 'Who is initiating the change you are about to make?' If it is someone else who is directing your future course, however much you love them, it is important to be sure that this is what you really want. Many a parent has, with the best motives, forced a child on a path to a career or marriage that seems right, but may deep down be a way of fulfilling their own unsatisfied dreams. It may seem best to follow the path of least resistance if we go with a partner to a job in another part of the country, move to a house near ageing relatives or turn down an opportunity to travel because friends persuade us we would miss home. Home may be where the heart is – and sometimes we can make innovations within a secure setting – but if you do turn down an opportunity, be sure that it is what you, not others, want.

Cen – the torch

The inner voice, inspiration, the inner flame, help in difficulty

Cen is one of the Fire Runes, the fire that burned in the great halls as well as more humble abodes and was fed with pine dipped in resin. The Anglo-Saxon poem talks of the torch burning 'where royal and noble folk rest inside the hall'.

As well as giving light, the torch could ignite the forge, the fire in the hearth or even a funeral pyre. It was sometimes used to kindle the Need Fire (the rune Nyd), which was lit at the great sun festivals. Without the torch, there is darkness, and without the inner flame, there is emptiness within.

But the other aspect of Fire is also present: the burnishing, cleansing aspect, the sacrificial as well as the celebratory flame, and it is the purgative effect that is emphasised in the Norse and Icelandic poems.

This is the cosmic fire from Muspelheim in the South, which met with ice from Niflheim in the North in the creation of the Norse world, but which would bring about the destruction of the old order of gods, the Aesir and Vanir. Its alter ego is Haegl, the rune of hail and the second element in creation. The appearance of these runes in a reading, or indeed any Fire and Ice runes together, indicates a fusion of opposites.

Cen in a reading

Cen may indicate that you have a decision to make and no clear pointers. There may be conflicting opinions flying round as to what your best course or future path should be, or someone may be misleading you. If you have doubts about the wisdom of a course of action or a piece of advice, however persuasive the person advocating it may be, listen to your own strong inner voice.

Believe in yourself and trust your own wisdom in the area or issue highlighted by other runes in your reading. Because of their intuitive natures, women have ready access to this inner source of wisdom, but may doubt their own powers. Think of the number of times you have listened to yourself, trusted your own counsel and been proved right, and your confidence in this potent source of knowledge will increase.

Because Cen is a Fire Rune, it is a symbol of illumination that may suddenly offer the solution to a long-standing problem or open your eyes to opportunities you had not considered. The answers may come while you are walking, or relaxing, in a dream, or if you look into the embers of a fire – even in a barbecue fire – you may see images that suggest the way forward.

You may find a new source of help and inspiration, perhaps in someone new in your life, or in a person whom you had not previously regarded as particularly wise or knowledgeable. This support may increase your understanding and open new avenues for you.

Hidden Cen

It is easy in the modern world to lose touch with our own inner guide, and in times of crisis to rely on experts – clairvoyants, psychologists or business advisers – to determine our destiny. While the opinion of others can give valuable input, we should not hand over our destiny to anyone, however wise. Doctors are increasingly recognising that mothers do know when their child is seriously ill, and this is an ability all women have, mothers or not: we can monitor our own well-being.

Hidden Cen says that you are perhaps doubting your own wisdom and relying on others to tell you the best course and to judge the rightness of your actions.

Whatever the issue to be considered, or decision to be made, or set of accounts to be balanced, stop and banish all conscious thought from your mind. The sibyl or prophetess at Cumae in ancient Rome, who would write the answers to questions on oak leaves and allow them to blow about in the wind so they became mixed up, was a wise lady. Step back from frantic activity, be quiet and alone and, above all, wait patiently. Hidden Cen marks the need to say and do nothing until the answer comes in its own time, like the torch illuminating darkness.

DAY 7

Gyfu – the gift

Generosity, all matters relating to exchanges, including contracts, love, marriage and sexual union

Gyfu is the rune of giving to others and unity, in sexuality and love, or more formally in marriage. It can also represent benevolence from a higher source, which may be a tangible blessing bestowed or knowledge and insight. It can also signify the exchange of favours or information.

This rune is not mentioned in the Old Norse or Icelandic rune poems, but the Anglo-Saxon poem presents a Christianised version of the blessings of giving and also of receiving if one is in need. In the old Norse tradition, a gift received required one to be given in return, and throughout history a gift has initiated a relationship with mutual obligations, so Gyfu is a rune that implies fair and considerate treatment by both parties in a relationship.

Hospitality and altruism were greatly valued as qualities by the Northern peoples. In the feudal and family-based society of the Nordic world, a person of property and recognition could confer status on an outcast by giving them land or animals, another aspect of Gyfu in the Anglo-Saxon poem.

Gyfu in a reading

Gyfu is often called the woman's rune and has direct parallels with the Empress card in the Tarot. For most women, whether they are part of a family unit or not, are natural givers – of time and care as well as material things – to those with whom they come into contact.

The appearance of Gyfu indicates a fruitful period for nurturing existing relationships and deepening new ones towards increasing commitment, for passion, for gaining satisfaction from giving and receiving love, and for mutual happiness. If the questioner is unattached, then great emotional satisfaction will be gained from developing friendships or from helping anyone who is vulnerable or in need. This may in itself open the door to future relationships. If anyone is in need of nurturing, then what is given will be returned threefold, not immediately but within months. Gifts and celebrations will bring pleasure.

Children and animals, whether your own or other people's, are also sources of satisfaction. This is one of the most positive runes, especially after an emotional setback or a period of loneliness, since it is the rune of unity, of bringing about reconciliation or new relationships.

Remember too, as the Anglo-Saxon poem says, that receiving is as creative as giving. Competent, caring women can sometimes find it hard to accept help or admit that they are feeling ill or worried. The greatest gift a mother can give her child is the ability to recognise and respond to the needs of others, beginning with her own. Successful career women can, by never showing vulnerability, unwittingly make others feel inadequate. Giving too much can be almost as bad as giving too little.

Hidden Gyfu

Because Gyfu is such a positive rune, its shadow side is equally potent. We all know the woman who gives everything to her family and feels neglected because no one shows her any gratitude. In spite of equality laws, the spectre of the ever-smiling wife, lover or mother still gleams from every advertisement. She is the woman who home-bakes apple pies, runs a merchant bank, meditates and works out in the gym every day; passionate, empathetic and with a marshmallow centre, however intellectual and competent she may be.

Quite illogically, many of us feel guilty and so push ourselves beyond the limits of our energies in the hope we will somehow attain that elusive seal of approval from our mothers, mothers-in-law, bosses, employees and children's teachers – we even crave the neighbours' admiration of our whiter-than-white washing. Hidden Gyfu frequently appears on women's readings along with hidden Nyd (the rune of needs). Once a seemingly successful author who was married to a wealthy businessman who seemed to adore her told me: 'I give to others what I need to be given myself'. Two years later, she was divorced. It is important to give to yourself the tolerance, kindness and nurturing you give to others.

DAY 8
Wyn – joy

Personal happiness, success and recognition of worth

Wyn represents happiness through oneself and one's own efforts rather than through others' achievement, and is often used as a focus for those needing success and tangible rewards for effort. To the Vikings, happiness meant having enough food, shelter and wealth and being accepted as part of a kin, but also experiencing the fulfilment that came through hardship in the exploration and conquest of uncharted lands. This rune appears only in the Anglo-Saxon poem, which equates the happy man with one who has 'power and blessedness' and knows few troubles (sometimes translated as 'knows a little' of troubles).

The second translation makes more sense, suggesting that it is those who have experienced some hardships who know the importance of taking happiness as it comes and, above all, finding personal joy through one's own actions, rather than expecting life to provide bounties.

Wyn in a reading

Wyn is one of the most fortunate runes to cast, being the rune of joy. Though others can make us happy and good fortune can ease our lives, ultimate happiness for each of us involves fulfilling our own unique destiny; this may be to travel, create beautiful objects, grow sunflowers, raise a family or develop our inner world – or a combination of all these and perhaps more. This rune is the other side of the coin to Gyfu and together they make an integrated whole, of others and self. For Wyn talks about the separate self as an individual, however fulfilling our relationships may be and however far we may be working towards a collective vision.

It may be cast at a natural time of change or crossroads in your life, or may mirror a growing awareness that pleasure as well as responsibilities, and spiritual or emotional fulfilment as well as material success, are necessary for contentment. You may have shed or be about to shed some responsibilities, or find yourself alone for a while and feel the need to explore your own identity. You may also reap the benefits of your work and efforts in the near future (more of this in the rune Ger).

Hidden Wyn

Your identity may have become blurred by a period of intense love or even difficulties in a relationship. Or, like some women, you may have spent so long considering the needs of others that you cannot remember what would make you happy. With family or friends, at work as well as socially, you have become the world's cheerleader, responsible for making sure everyone has a good time, while you go home with a headache. Or you may have worked so hard because of the need to pay a mortgage and bills, or because a project was vital to the success of your company or necessary for your career, that you have forgotten how to relax, and feel guilty if you discover you are enjoying yourself.

Now is time to redress the balance and get your inner self back on course, to be rather than do, to dream rather than talk or act. Do something, however small, to make yourself happy every day and rediscover the small joys that make life worthwhile.

Casting the runes

Now that you have learned the first rune row, you are ready to begin casting the runes on your cloth. With a relatively small number of runes, you may not get a truly representative reading. Nevertheless, even with the first eight runes you can gain insight into a specific question or issue: the meanings of the runes cast, the areas of the cloth in which they fall, whether the marked or blank side is uppermost and finally if they fall in a cluster or separately – these are all significant.

The circle method detailed below is one I used in my book *Crystals Talk to the Woman Within*, although the areas of the cloth are named differently, as it is a form of casting that has historical roots with several systems. The meanings of the circles in both systems are virtually identical and if you have learned both the crystals and runes, a joint reading can often show parallels in significance between specific crystals and runes.

Each area of the casting cloth represents a different level of experience, or realm; by interpreting runes that fall in each realm, you can understand more clearly the relationship between the stones and pinpoint specific areas of your life where positive energy or input is available or needed.

+ Sit in the moonlight if possible as you work. The Full Moon is especially potent for creating runes. If the Moon is not visible, light red candles at the four main compass positions. A shaded lamp can supplement the light for working.

+ Choose a piece of fabric about 50 cm (20 in) square in a pale colour; white is excellent and traditional, as you can see the runes against it. A plain square scarf is ideal.

+ First, find the centre of the cloth, then draw three concentric circles, using a red marker pen. The easiest way is to draw around three inverted plates in size order, the smallest first; use one the size of a saucer for the innermost circle, followed by a tea plate and finally a dinner plate. Alternatively, you can use a pair of compasses. As long as you have an area of unmarked cloth about 10 cm (4 in) around the outside of the largest circle, you need not be exact. The first circle will have a radius of about 6.25 cm (2½ in), the second about 12.5 cm (5 in) and the third about 18. 75 cm (7 in).

✤ Experiment on paper until you produce the right format and cast runes on to it to see whether the dimensions work in practice. You may create a cloth for your own work and a second for reading for others. Note, I have suggested using red for my markings as this is the colour associated with runic divination, but you can use black or any colour that shows clearly.

✤ You can, if you wish, sew red running stitches around each circle, as you do so visualising the wisdom and intuition of the Moon entering your cloth, filling it with positive energies.

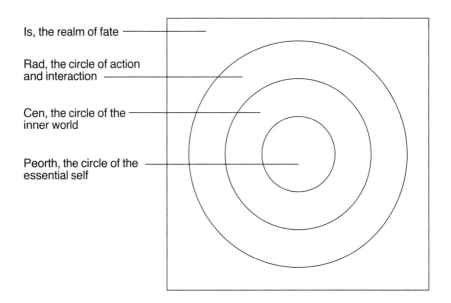

Is, the realm of fate

Rad, the circle of action and interaction

Cen, the circle of the inner world

Peorth, the circle of the essential self

Peorth, the circle of the essential self

Peorth is a rune you will meet later that represents the essential unchanging core you have within you that makes you uniquely yourself. Its subsidiary meaning is Fate, and refers to the fate you create yourself from your personal blueprint.

The innermost circle talks of the core issues in life, fundamental beliefs, the essential person you were as a small child before the world intruded, who remains basically unchanged throughout all the stages of womanhood. So this circle marks the boundaries of you, the individual, as opposed to you and a lover, or you with family, friends or colleagues; the person you are after everyone else has gone away or is asleep, who sits alone, but is not lonely, the complete and separate you, body, mind and soul.

Runes that fall in this area are of great significance in both the immediate and long-term future and usually suggest independent action or an original solution.

Here, too, lies your untapped potential, your personal evolutionary blueprint for worldly, intellectual or spiritual development, which unfolds gradually throughout your life and may be modified by circumstance or others, but which always retains your personal hallmark.

Through developing these potential personal destinies, rather than following blind fate or other people, you will automatically attain ever higher levels of awareness so that you experience deeper pleasure and insight even in quite mundane moments and start to understand the patterns of existence and your own place in this interconnected universe.

If the blank faces of runes fall here frequently, you may be out of touch with your true self and may be trying to adapt yourself to the expectations of others. You may need time to be, rather than to do, and the space to reconnect with your centre.

Cen, the circle of the inner world

Cen is the rune of the inner flame and the voice associated with the inner world of your dreams and insights. The middle circle is the circle of thoughts and emotions, where conscious and unconscious worlds meet, where reason and intuition can work in harmony, bringing together the left and right sides of the brain into an integrated whole.

Runes that fall here indicate that it is a time to formulate plans and listen to dreams that may hold solutions and initiate new paths. Our minds are never still and your psychic antennae may already be tuning into future opportunities or deep-seated desires that may be expressed as specific needs or plans, not immediately, but in the weeks or even months ahead.

For this is the area least troubled by constraints of space and time, where you can rehearse endings and beginnings, achieve successes, win battles and master unfamiliar processes. What is more, by the mysterious and largely untapped powers of the mind and psyche, using the powers of visualisation (focused imagination) and empowerments or mantras (concentrated declarations of intent), you can transfer power to bring about the manifestation of dreams and desires in the outer world.

Our inner voice can be our most accurate guide to action if we listen to it. It can filter out those superfluous but strident voices that give conflicting advice; these may be voices from the past that linger within our head or the opinions of those presently around us. It can warn us of potential hazards, such as untrustworthy people or situations that may on the surface appear reliable. Conversely, this inner voice may offer reassurance if the future seems uncertain.

Runes in this circle can reinforce the rightness of decisions we were contemplating and help us to separate our innate wisdom from the free-floating anxieties that dull imagination and block rational planning.

Blank runes here indicate that you may be relying too much on the judgement of others and doubting your own wisdom and knowledge.

Rad, the circle of action and interaction

Rad is the rune of the wheel and of movement of all kinds and so is an excellent rune to represent the area of action and relationships, not only with lovers and partners, but also with family, friends, colleagues and officialdom.

Runes cast here indicate interaction with others, communication, negotiations, persuading others to your point of view, or adapting your plans or actions, without losing sight of the inner person of the first circle or the dreams of the second. It is the realm of putting your thoughts and plans into action and of making tangible progress towards material success, personal happiness or resolving problems.

So whether you are initiating a new venture or embarking on a fresh stage of your life, declaring love or saying goodbye, sending your book to a publisher, planning a holiday or spring-cleaning your life, and whether you are 18 or 80, the open road of life is calling. You should seize any opportunities for new experiences, meet new people, try new activities and aim high, especially if you have a number of marked runes in this circle.

Hidden runes in your circle of action indicate that the spring-cleaning aspect should come to the fore: you may need to shed burdens that you need no longer carry, but do so out of habit. Consider what changes would bring happiness to you (as opposed to those around you). Even if your options are limited, maximise whatever opportunities you have and try to take a small step each day towards fulfilling your own goals.

Is, the realm of fate

Any runes that fall on the cloth outside the three circles fall into Is, the realm of ice and what is yet to come.

Is, or Ice, was the fifth element in the Viking world and so is a potent rune representing those events that are for now waiting outside your present world, but will soon enter when the time is right. Over the years I have modified the way I interpreted this area beyond the circles. At one time I would read all runes that fell outside the circles, even if they were on the floor or table, as though they had fallen within Is. But I have obtained far more accurate readings since I have disregarded those that fall beyond its realm.

I now cast another rune to replace any that fall off the cloth and in practice the new rune may land anywhere and like all unexpected factors change the tenet of the reading. The more runes needed to complete the three, six or nine cast that you will carry out, the more fluid the situation and you may benefit from a second rune cast a few days later to see what is moving into your life.

The runes that fall outside the three circles but remain on the cloth in this outer segment of Is, especially if they are hidden, are of great significance.

In the Viking world, where ice and snow would make travelling impossible, people had to wait for the ice to melt, so resting and becoming stronger by the time spring came. Modern heating and lighting turn night into day and winter into summer, and our bodies and spirits suffer from the loss of the darker days when people would rest and sleep more and, on a spiritual level, that is what this segment is recommending.

So the realm of Is represents what is soon to be moving into the questioner's life and runes in this area suggest that inaction is the best course, until the ice melts naturally to allow events to unfold that may affect your future plans. This can, in a sense, represent the most difficult area of all, perhaps accepting that a long-awaited move, at home or at work, or a desire to begin again, must be delayed, that it is not the time to initiate change or to speak out. But equally it can be a very fruitful area, a time of allowing seeds to take root and ideas to germinate.

If runes are hidden here, however, it can suggest that you are keeping yourself static and you should examine whether you are avoiding change through fear or because you do not really want it.

Casting the runes:
an alternative method

Runes were still publicly cast by tribes and individuals in the Northern lands for divinatory purposes until the eleventh century and the last Rune Masters and Mistresses did not die out until about 300 years ago.

The tradition they followed dates back hundreds of years, perhaps much longer. The first recorded rune castings are described by the Roman author Tacitus in his *Germania*, written in about 98 CE (Common Era), recording the customs of the ancient Germanic peoples. Tacitus recounted that a white cloth was used for throwing rune 'staves' and that a branch would be cut from a nut-bearing tree and rune markings etched into strips of the bark to make staves. These staves were cast and interpreted either by a priest or the father of the family or clan, who, Tacitus says, 'offered a prayer to the gods and, looking up to the sky, picked up three strips, one at a time and read their meaning from the signs previously scored on them'. Tacitus also records that women were involved in augury of all kinds.

You can use the rune stave method, either buying the staves or creating them from 30 even-sized twigs of oak or ash, picked if possible just before sunset, the beginning of the Northern day. Scrape away the bark at the top and etch or use an engraving tool or penknife to cut the symbol on each and paint it red. Leave the thirtieth stave blank. My own rune staves were made by cutting a wooden curtain rail into equal sections. Keep the rune staves in a long drawstring bag, made of a natural fabric, or a long metal tin, so that you can shake them before casting.

Casting the rune staves

Rune staves are traditionally cast at sunset or sunrise beneath any tree, preferably an oak or ash tree.

+ Draw a circle with a circumference of approximately 100 cm (40 in) in black or red on a square or sheet of white cloth, so that there is a plain area about 30 cm (12 in) deep around the circle.

+ Secure the sheet to the ground with large stones at each of the corners.

+ Alternatively, draw your circle directly into the soil with any stick you can find.

+ You can, if you wish, formulate a question or ask the person for whom you are reading to ask a question. However, the most effective rune stave readings tend to be ones where you allow your mind to go blank, as you cast the runes.

+ Kneel or sit about 100 cm (40 in) away from the cloth. Either take the lid off your tin and shake it, allowing the staves to scatter on the cloth or, holding all the staves between your clasped hands, fling them outwards and upwards in the direction of the cloth.

+ Ignore any staves or runes that fall outside the circle, whether these are on the cloth or on the ground.

+ Read only those runes that fall face uppermost and if you have all blank runes then leave the reading for another day.

Psychic protection

Once you begin rune divination, you will be open to all kinds of psychic energies as your psyche unfolds. The majority of these will be entirely benign. Psychic protection is rather like giving your e-mail address or phone number only to those whom you wish to contact you, rather than placing your name in a public directory. If you carry out rune divination or rituals only when you feel positive and try to see the best in any situation or person, you have inbuilt protection, for everything is said to return threefold to the sender. But if you read runes for others or are surrounded, as we all are at one time and another, by hostility or apathy, it can be helpful to protect yourself as you work, from your own buried negativity as well as that of others. In my work with crystals and Tarot cards, I have found other methods that are effective, but this is one that seems particularly potent for runic work.

Creating sentinels of light

The Scandinavian peoples believed in the ancient concept of earth dwights, tall shadowy presences who stood sentinel over areas of land and villages, protecting them at night; these protective guardians drew power from Mother Earth, or Nerthus as she was also known. Others visualise these protective presences as angels or beings of light who symbolically draw around you the benevolence of the universal power of the cosmos or the protective god or goddess with whom you identify.

✛ First, either use a compass to find the magnetic north of your home or use a symbolic point based on the approximate geographical direction of north.

✛ Locate the four main compass positions in the room in which you carry out your private rune work.

✣ Place candle brackets near these spots on four walls. Alternatively, position four tall purple or dark blue candles in the four positions around the room at 12, 3, 6 and 9 o'clock, placing your 12 o'clock candle in the north. (There are many excellent tall pillar candles on the market.)

✣ As dusk falls, make a circle of your runes in order, light each of your candles beginning with the candle in the north and stand within the circle of runes, facing north.

✣ Focus first on the candle in the north, which represents the element of Earth and Midnight, and with your legs together, raise your arms diagonally above your head, to form a V shape. Actually making the letters with the body was a powerful form of runic magic. You have created the shape of Eohl, the rune of Higher Powers. Say:

Guardians of the North, protect me against any who would do me harm, intentionally or unintentionally.

✣ Next, face the east and raising your arms as before to create Eohl once more with your body, say:

Guardians of the East, protect me against any who would do me harm, intentionally or unintentionally.

✣ Now, face the south and make the Eohl for the third time, saying,

Guardians of the South, protect me against any who would do me harm, intentionally or unintentionally.

✣ Finally, face the west and create the Eohl, saying,

Guardians of the West, protect me against any who would do me harm, intentionally or unintentionally.

✣ Visualise the protective light joining each of the guardians to form an unbroken circle.

✣ Make a gesture as you stand bathed in light, for example draw a circle on your palm and say,

When I make this sign, the Guardians of the Four Quarters will protect me within this circle of light.

✦ Blow or snuff out the candles, beginning in the west and proceeding anti-clockwise, and visualise the circle of light fading gradually, but not disappearing.

✦ The candle guardians can be activated whenever you need them by making your special sign, but you should renew the protective circle regularly by lighting the candles and recreating the circle. Once a month, on or close to the night of the Full Moon, light the four candles around the circle of runes and leave them to burn right down until they go out.

DAY 9
Haegl – hail

Disruption by natural events and uncontrolled forces, sudden change

Haegl belongs to the second set of runes that we shall look at, the aett of Haegl or Heimdall, watcher of the gods. It is known as the Mother Rune, in the position of the sacred number nine. In its original shape as the six-pointed snowflake, Haegl had a geometric form found in the composition of many natural forms of life. Haegl, the hailstone, is regarded as the cosmic seed, for Ice was the second main element involved in creation and as such Haegl is the alter ego of Cen. The Old Norse rune poem speaks of hail as 'the coldest of grains', associating it with the harvest, for when hail melts, it becomes life-giving water. Haegl speaks of the cold world beyond the shelter of the homestead. The Anglo-Saxon poem emphasises the potential new life and the promise of spring within Haegl.

Haegl has therefore come to represent sudden change, whether determined by external events or a decision to initiate change that may be unwelcome to others.

Haegl in a reading

When we cast Haegl, it may indicate that we feel we are out in the cold, perhaps at work or in our personal life. Or we may realise that we need to cause disruption, stand out against an unfair or unsatisfactory situation. We may need to make a change that is right for us, but which others may resist because it disturbs the predictable, familiar image we offer that keeps them secure and unchallenged. 'Stay just as you are' may sound romantic when you are sweet 16 and your knight in shining armour has galloped up and promised you eternal blue skies, fountains flowing with wine and not a dirty sock in sight – echoes of Rad. But now you are wiser, stronger, more focused and in need of a partner, friends and colleagues who can grow with you and encourage you to explore different facets of yourself – not take you for granted as the rock upon which they shelter from life's storms.

Haegl is not always welcomed in a rune cast or in our lives. And yet it speaks of transformation, of moving on from the stagnation of Is, the third rune in this set, and one that frequently accompanies it, towards movement. New life is there waiting for you as ice melts from around your heart and releases your power to turn setbacks into advantage – as long as you refuse to accept second-best in any aspect of your life. This rune says that you are worth so much more, so let the logic of Air cut through any opposition, doubts or fears.

Whether the change you need or seek is small or large, the seed of creation is within you. Women are especially good in adversity or challenging situations. So be courageous and, unlike those warriors in the Rad rune who sat in their halls, waiting for the snow and hail to cease, meet life head-on, and reap the benefits in the sunnier days to follow.

Hidden Haegl

Disruption is, typically, guys' stuff: think of all that macho chest-thumping if his report isn't ready, his shirt hasn't magically washed and ironed itself, or when the match is cancelled because of rain. Women tend to smooth down the crises: they know that life isn't a bed of roses, that into each life a lot of rain and hail will fall, that trains are late and children fall ill at the most inconvenient times. So it is a question of putting up the umbrella and sailing forth regardless rather than complaining about what cannot be changed.

Maybe that's why we women enjoy escapist romantic films. Women tend to absorb the extra demands, the additional workload caused by unexpected crises and expand time to fill the needs. To protest, to give way to illness or PMT, to complain when life or loved ones offer shoddy service, is not what nice girls do.

I have known powerful women who drive themselves to the point of exhaustion in the field of business, who will just smile weakly when an adolescent daughter lies in bed 'exhausted' after a hard weekend socialising while the home is in chaos, or who protest only mildly if service is slow and unhelpful in a restaurant or the washing machine man fails to call when they've taken a second afternoon off work, because his van wasn't working or his aunt has unexpectedly come over from Australia.

But remember it does not have to be like that. The world will not stop if we step off for a while or make demands of others that will disrupt their smooth pathways through life at our expense – so try it and feel the hail melt into brilliant sunbeams.

DAY 10
Nyd – need

Needs that can be met – by action and reaction to external events, self-reliance, the desire for achievement, passion

Nyd, the second Fire Rune, is another of the cosmic forces that is recognised as being a shaping power in the creation of the world and the fate of mankind. It is the spindle that kindled the Need Fire by friction rather than from external flame. Nyd Fires were lit from early times all over Northern Europe on festivals such as Beltane, (May Eve), the beginning of Summer, Samhain (Halloween), and on the Solstices. Even today, Christian Easter Eve ceremonies of burning the Judas Man and rekindling the paschal candle are held in parts of Germany and Eastern Europe.

These were fires of new life and light, whose ashes fertilised the fields and persuaded the sun to shine again. And it is the inner Nyd Fire that drives a woman to obtain that which she most desires. Because of this Nyd is associated with love magic.

The Old Norse poem makes the link between Fire and Ice, the Nyd Fire being kindled against the frost and cold, while the Anglo-Saxon poem likens it to a tight band on the chest, which can be turned into an omen of help if attended early. So it is a very exciting rune to cast, promising fulfilment and warmth if we attend to our own needs.

Nyd in a reading

The Nyd rune will appear when you want something (or someone) passionately, the feeling like a tight band that can only be released by striving for the object you desire. It may be a dream as yet unfulfilled or one long buried, for a spiritual goal or for success, joy, travel or love. Recently the dream may have become more focused or have been rekindled by events or simply the stage of your life. It may be that you have to build up to happiness in a small way, like the candles at Easter, being lit one by one.

Your Nyd may have changed and evolved, and for the first time you may be clear about a new direction or perhaps allowing your own needs, as opposed to the needs of those around you, to take priority. It may begin with reading a book, travelling to somewhere different, making positive efforts to get to know someone who makes you feel alive, or the kindling or rekindling of passion within a relationship. Or you may answer the call to pull up your roots, move home or perhaps just set up your own home in the way that makes you fulfilled.

Hidden Nyd

Your needs may not be met by other people and you may feel you are always giving in your relationships or at work, and now you need attention or recognition of your worth. Hidden Nyd often appears with hidden Gyfu. We can at first disregard our own needs because of the demands of career or family, but it can become a habit long after the original need for altruism is outgrown. People can genuinely be unaware that we have unfulfilled needs because we have never voiced them. Giving indiscriminately can cramp our own development.

Because the Nyd Fire is usually kindled by friction of two pieces of wood without any external fuel, it suggests action rather than a passive response and rekindling the fire of enthusiasm within yourself, especially on dark, dull winter days. If there is no one in your life who can or will give to you, fulfil your own needs, a little each day, and learn to rekindle the fires within yourself.

DAY 11
Is – ice

*Obstruction, a period of inactivity which can be turned to
advantage, waiting for the right moment*

Is is the second Ice Rune and the fifth element in the Norse world.
The single vertical form of the rune means that it is contained
within every other rune, again a cosmic seed. It is described in the
Norse poem as a 'broad bridge' and in the Icelandic verse as 'roof
of the waves'. The Anglo-Saxon poem refers to Ice as 'most like a
jewel and fair to see' so it is a very positive rune.

Is can be seen as the ice of winter that in the Far North freezes
even the sea over and stops hunting and exploration, an external
obstacle to movement. This pause allows time for reflection, rest
or planning. In the modern world we have lost touch with the
seasons and the natural slowing down and restoration for the
body and mind, offered by dark winter days.

Is is also the icy glacier flowing imperceptibly from Niflheim, the
realm of Ice, indicating progress that seems slow but is occurring
beneath the surface.

Is in a reading

When this rune is cast, you may be feeling frustrated that matters
are progressing slowly or that you are unable to act or begin a new
project. Is says that it may be a time to wait for the right moment
and, above all, to slow down when possible so that you have the
impetus to make a surge forward when the ice melts.

It can be dispiriting to have applied for 20 jobs and have had no response, to have enrolled on a course only to find that practical obstacles make it difficult for you to study or attend classes. Perhaps a relationship cannot progress because you are waiting for a divorce or for the attitudes of others to soften; you cannot find a cheap enough flat to leave home or a family member is ill or a partner needs your attention and support.

There are a thousand scenarios at work and in your personal world when you have done everything you can towards being promoted, moving home, even arranging a holiday, only to find circumstances apparently conspiring to frustrate your efforts. At such a time you must accept that this is not the moment to move forward; instead try to make every day of waiting pleasurable or creative even in a small way until the right time comes when the ice will melt. This waiting time can be a very positive period spiritually, if you do not dissipate energies on resentments or unrealistic time scales.

Hidden Is

A subsidiary meaning of Is indicates a need to negotiate carefully the 'ice bridge' spanning the dimensions. Hidden Is talks about the fear of falling and also the fear of failure, a recurring theme among hidden runes that may keep us in a less than satisfactory situation. The fear is often worse than the reality and your heart may be frozen by previous betrayal or your initiative by an earlier setback. Perhaps others have eroded your self-confidence and so every time you go to make that new beginning you draw back in fear. As time goes on, the fears magnify and the ice thickens so that they become distorted and out of all proportion to the original loss. Be kind to yourself, but gently and gradually melt the ice and negotiate the way forward; take care, but also have courage.

DAY 12
Ger – the year

Harvest: the results of earlier efforts realised, life cycles that can be fruitful or a repetition of old mistakes

Ger represents the natural progression through the cycles of existence, from season to season, from year to year, through the stages of life or in a specific relationship or situation. This rune of good harvest or completion of endeavour is invoked in magic ritual and may be held as a talisman for a good season or project.

Both the Norse and Icelandic poems refer to a good harvest being to the profit of all men and the Norse poem talks of the generosity of Frey, or Ingwaz, the god of fertility of the land, whose wagon was driven across the fields in a ceremony of fertilising the fields. The Anglo-Saxon poem promises 'bright abundance' for rich and poor and so, at its most positive, Ger is a rune heralding prosperity and increase.

Ger in a reading

Ger represents fertility of all kinds, the ability to achieve any goal by hard work and the need to nourish projects through dedicated input to fruitful completion. The rune is a version of the words of the Bible, 'As you sow, shall you reap', and so this rune promises that any past endeavours, whether for love, success, prosperity or joy, will be fulfilled in the near future.

As the rune of the harvest, Ger is a symbol of autumn and so represents a time of assessment of the past and plans for the future. You may need to consider long-term financial matters and investments and also pay attention to family affairs, especially encouraging younger or weaker members towards their goals and reconciling long-standing quarrels or bitterness. For women, through their association with the Earth Goddess, Ger represents wisdom, maturity and harmony with their female reproductive cycles, whether they are physically fertile or not. You should go forward, confident that you are on the right path and that, whatever the focus of your life, you will reap rich rewards.

Hidden Ger

Ger is linked with the life cycle as the great solar wheel of the world turns, with one season succeeding another. And so we need to pass from one stage of our life to the next, knowing when it is time to close one door and open another. In popular tradition, Ger is sometimes called the treadmill rune. It may appear when you are constantly trapped in the same repetitive cycle, like a hamster on the wheel. So it is possible to find ourselves repeating destructive relationship scenarios every five years, although with different people, or encountering similar career problems over and over again at different stages of life. It is important if there are recurring patterns in your life to examine the reasons that you draw back at the moment of commitment or chance for success. Does the same kind of guy or woman always make you unhappy or move out when difficulties strike?

Hidden Ger says that the past should be examined and self-defeating patterns shed. You deserve more than a re-run of old movies with sad endings – rewrite the script and become the heroine.

Choosing your rune of the day

I mentioned earlier that one of the reasons for keeping a journal was so that you could note your selected rune of the day, to see if over a period of days a particular rune or runes kept appearing, which would suggest that certain areas of your life needed attention or that specific opportunities were coming your way. Recurring runes over a period of days or weeks tap into the same process that causes a recurring dream.

Now that you have learned to read 12 runes, you can begin to choose a rune of the day each morning to give you the overall mood of the day and suggest strengths and strategies you can use to maximise opportunities and minimise potential difficulties.

✛ Select your rune first thing in the morning from your bag. Place your hand inside the bag and let it guide you to the appropriate rune. You can focus on a particular issue if you wish, or allow your unconscious wisdom to guide you.

✛ Some women cast the rune to see whether the blank or marked side falls uppermost, but others allow the whole rune to speak and incorporate both meanings, the marked side as opportunities or strengths and the blank side as challenges. This avoids having purely challenging aspects as your focus for the day.

✛ You may wish to buy or sew a small red silk bag in which to carry your rune of the day as an amulet of protection and power. Cleanse the rune if you have a bad day by sprinkling a few grains of salt over it and passing it through a candle flame.

✛ When you have nine days' readings, you can study the overall pattern as Veronica did in the reading overleaf. You may prefer to carry out a weekly analysis. As the weeks pass, look back over a month and see if you can detect recurring patterns: is a particular rune associated, for example, with Monday morning or the day you visit your daughter-in-law?

✛ Though runes are as likely to confirm that you are on the right track as to reveal problems, they are a potent way of coming up with solutions that may have eluded you on a conscious level. It is rather like retaining and examining your dreams, which often hold answers but are elusive and too quickly forgotten.

Veronica's rune of the day reading

This reading is based on runes chosen on nine consecutive days. For her daily rune selection, Veronica used a full set of 30 runes, including the blank rune of Odin or the destiny you have yet to fulfil. But as all the runes she drew are those that we have already looked at, it is well worth studying her reading.

Her experience is one that is increasingly common at a time when a third of marriages end in divorce and an increasing number of families include a step-parent. We all know about the wicked step-mother myth, but it can often be step-fathers who find difficulty in adapting to a new family, especially if they have not experienced fatherhood before.

Veronica is in her mid-thirties and has three children aged six, eight and thirteen. She has recently married for the second time after a traumatic divorce caused by her first husband's constant womanising and unwillingness to be responsible for the children. Joe, her second husband, was a bachelor and, though he loves Veronica, he finds it hard to come to terms with the noise and mess of family life. Even with her part-time job, Veronica experiences persistent financial worry as her ex-husband pays little maintenance to her, though he showers the children with expensive gifts on the rare occasions he sees them.

There seems to be a constant running battle between Joe and the children, especially the teenager, and Veronica finds herself caught in the middle; the children also play Joe off against her ex-husband. Veronica has a permanent headache and, dearly though she loves them all as individuals, some days she feels like walking out and leaving them all to their battles.

Veronica casts each rune on to the table and so differentiates between the positive and blank side. Her runes are:

Day 1: Haegl   **Day 6: Gyfu (hidden)**

Day 2: Thorn   **Day 7: Feoh**

Day 3: Feoh (hidden)   **Day 8: Gyfu (hidden)**

Day 4: Thorn   **Day 9: Haegl (hidden)**

Day 5: Ger (hidden)

Veronica begins and ends on Haegl (hail), though the second one is hidden. Not surprisingly, she is surrounded by a lot of aggravation from other people, not least the running battle between her second husband and the children; the situation is aggravated by her ex-husband and his lavish gifts, coupled with his sporadic and inadequate practical and financial support. The disruption mirrored in Haegl consists mainly of everyday irritations and quarrels over the way the children behave.

Thorn (thorns) on Day 2 indicates that the tension is building up. Veronica is already experiencing headaches. Thorn is repeated on Day 4, showing that the irritations and petty battles are a continuous, wearing feature of Veronica's life.

Hidden Ger (the harvest) on Day 5 suggests that feeling caught in the centre of others' quarrels is a characteristic of Veronica's life, perhaps carried over from her first marriage – or even her childhood. It is probable that in her first marriage, like many women, Veronica hid the problems so successfully that the children now regard her ex-husband as a super-hero. Veronica should ask herself why she continues to take on the Cinderella role, especially as the handsome prince has turned into one of the warring peasants.

Gyfu (the gift) is hidden on both Day 6 and Day 8, suggesting that Veronica is perhaps assuming the giving role all the time because she feels that to do otherwise would make her a bad mother and wife. What is worse, she fears it would result in her second husband leaving her, as did his predecessor. Veronica has unrealistic expectations, based on the popular image of the happy family, and feels responsible because hers, like 95 per cent of real-life units, has as many quarrels as moments of domestic bliss.

Day 7 brings Feoh, the price to be paid, in this case the price of continuing the way things are: hostility from her present husband and her children and a destructive attitude in her ex-husband. Of course there is the underlying price to be paid for change: losing her perception of herself as super-mum. In addition there is her deepest fear, that she may lose Joe, who has found the realities of family life so different from his solo existence and his own idealised picture of the happy family.

The final hidden Haegl on Day 9 suggests that Veronica is avoiding protesting that her home is being turned into a war zone and that this is no longer acceptable.

Before you read on, write down your own interpretation of Veronica's runes and the solution they suggest. Then read my understanding of their significance, remembering that each of us reads the runes in our own way and that the most accurate interpretation is Veronica's own.

To me, the runes seem to be indicating that Veronica needs to remove herself, not from her home (tempting though it is), but from standing in the middle of the confrontations, for while she is absorbing the impact of the arguments, the combatants do not need to make any changes in their attitude or behaviour. Of course, it is never easy when a step-parent moves into a family, especially when the absent father, who previously may never have given the children a kind word, becomes, on his departure, Father Christmas and St Joseph combined.

If the children are old enough to be manipulative, they are old enough to bear the consequences of their behaviour, and Joe too will adapt to family life if he is exposed to it, rather than being protected and allowed to assume the role of indulged child instead of responsible parent. The situation may not have a happy ending – real life sometimes does not – but once Veronica is aware of her own unconscious collusion in the conflict, the differences can be faced and hopefully resolved.

A cast of three runes

Although you have learned only 12 runes, you can begin to cast those you know. Since all the runes are related to our lives, even an apparently unrepresentative set of 12 will shed insight on any question you ask. However, you can, if you prefer, wait until you have learned all the runes before adopting the casting method.

The method is the same, whether you cast three, six or nine runes, according to the complexity of the issue under consideration. A three-rune reading is very effective if you do not have much time or want to consider a specific matter.

✢ Place the marked runes in the bag and, as you hold it, concentrate on an issue or question, or if there is nothing specific that concerns you, allow your mind to go blank, visualising a starry sky with the stars fading one by one to create a velvet darkness.

✢ Using your power hand (the one you write with), touch the runes inside the bag one by one; take your time, allowing the ones that feel right to remain in your hand. Draw the three chosen runes out together.

✢ Cast the three runes from your hand in a single movement on to your casting cloth. If any fall outside the cloth, substitute another from the bag until you have three runes to read.

✢ Note the positions of the runes in relation to each other. Do they form a cluster? This would suggest they are related. Has one landed on top, dominating the others? Or have they scattered to corners of the cloth, suggesting different influences or choices?

✢ The realms in which they land are also of significance. If, for example, the runes fall in Cen, the realm of your inner world, the issue may be confined to your thoughts, something you are planning that is keeping you awake at night.

✣ Study any hidden runes. Why are they hidden? If all three are blank face uppermost, there may be a lot of unresolved business, so be gentle with yourself and those you read for.

✣ If you are reading the runes for someone else, ask them to hold the bag, think of the question and cast three together on to the cloth.

✣ You can then interpret the rune meanings according to the different areas and work with the questioner to determine how the chosen runes offer solutions to the situation under consideration. Do not be drawn into a psychic guessing game: spontaneous insights on your part will come more easily when you are relaxed and not under pressure to perform.

Eleanor's cast of three

This is an actual cast of three that I helped Eleanor to interpret, using the full set of runes.

Eleanor is in her mid-twenties and has worked for the same firm since she left school. She has a good position with responsibility for customer care. However, she is bored and finds herself having less patience than previously when dealing with the complaints from the public that form the core of her work. Recently she has spent more and more of her free time working on animal paintings and has accepted several commissions to paint or draw people's pets.

She has been seriously considering going freelance, but her parents point out that if she does so, she will never be able to afford the deposit on the flat she is contemplating buying and will have to remain in her cramped rented bedsitter.

Eleanor casts

Rune 1: Rad, hidden in Cen, the circle of her inner world

Rune 2: Feoh, in Rad, the outer circle of action and interaction

Rune 3: Thorn, in Is, outside the other circles, in the realm of fate, or what is yet to come

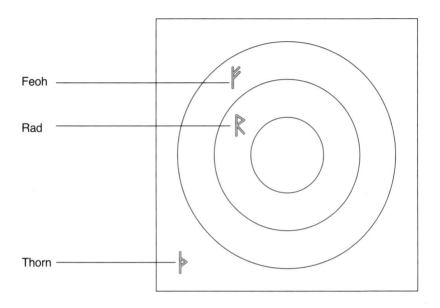

The circles help to pinpoint the meaning of each rune more clearly.

Rad, the wheel, which is concerned with a challenging but exciting decision involving change and movement, is in Eleanor's thoughts, but it is hidden. This indicates that Eleanor is finding it hard to make any positive steps in the real world, so it all goes round and round in her mind. There are hidden fears of failure and of giving up her secure, if unsatisfying, world. There is also the suggestion that in the past she has allowed others to dictate her course.

Feoh says that the price Eleanor must pay for change is a heavy one. If she wants to turn a hobby into a career she will have to cope with opposition from her parents, financial risk, extra work in the transitional stage as she struggles to balance two careers and all the new demands that will be made on her if she works for herself. But she is still young and it will be much harder to get off the financial treadmill once she has a mortgage and commitments.

The third rune, Thorn in Is, is perhaps the key. The small irritations are there and they are building up, making Eleanor feel trapped: the monotony of the job, the lack of scope for development within it and the constant inevitable negative feedback from her clients. Now may not be the ideal time to act. However, if Eleanor does not do something about her feelings of being trapped and try to melt the ice to bring positive change into her life, she may lose her incentive to make a more fulfilling life for herself. Worse, if the tensions accumulate she may even walk out of her secure job over something trivial, rather than leaving in a carefully planned career move.

The fate of the runes, as I said earlier, is not fixed, but depends upon our actions and reactions. I met Eleanor about three years after the original reading. Initially she had built up a part-time artistic business, while reducing her hours at work through a job-share. Ironically, she said, this brought her former enthusiasm back to her customer care work and she realised that she did enjoy working with people.

When I last saw Eleanor she was embarking on a training course in occupational therapy and was helping at the local hospital on a voluntary basis, teaching long-term patients with disabilities to paint. She had met Joel, one of the nurses in the long-stay section, and they were planning to set up home together.

Eoh – the yew

Endings leading to new beginnings, permanence, fidelity, wisdom in the later years, tradition

Because the yew is the longest-living tree, it was adopted by the Northern peoples as a symbol of longevity, tradition and eternal life, and was frequently placed where ashes or bones were buried to transfer its immortality to the deceased.

Sacred to Ullr, god of winter and archery, who lived in a grove of sacred yews, this was the tree of shamans and magic, burned as the sacred yule at the midwinter solstice to persuade the sun to return. As an evergreen it is called in the Norse rune poem 'the greenest wood in the winter' and in the Anglo-Saxon poem it is referred to as the fire's guardian and a joy to the home, providing warmth and promise that the trees will be green in the spring.

The rune Eoh is associated in the Icelandic poem with the bow, often made from yew wood, as a symbol of new life springing from the old; Yr, the bow, is a rune in the final row of the Anglo-Saxon runes. Eoh also represents lasting emotions and so fidelity in relationships.

Eoh in a reading

This rune may appear when you are contemplating an ending or have experienced one and are still uncertain about the future. When one avenue closes, a new opportunity invariably follows; one stage in a relationship may be naturally ending and something new is needed to cope with transitions.

The unique message of the yew is that we should accept that although we may feel sad or apprehensive at a transition, a promise of new, more permanent growth, success or happiness is inbuilt in the rune meaning.

You may find yourself alone by choice or necessity. Your family may have fled the nest; you may be facing retirement, redundancy, moving to a new area or even anticipating a new job or the birth of a first child that marks the end of a separate existence.

Even the most positive and exciting new beginnings may involve closing other doors. Allow yourself to express negative emotions rather than repressing them. A new world, big or small, is waiting, but you may feel anxiety mingled with the anticipation and should acknowledge this. If you have doubts about someone's fidelity, express it in a non-confrontational way and seek the reassurance you need.

Most important is the awareness that whatever you were promised when you began your adult life path, you cannot have it all, and if you want to succeed then you may have to forfeit leisure or activities you once enjoyed. One woman who consistently cast this rune admitted regretting that since her promotion she could no longer play her guitar to professional level in the evenings. However, she came to realise she could still play for pleasure in her spare time, so that one day, when pressures eased, she might resume playing professionally.

Hidden Eoh

These unrealistic expectations keep the fortune-tellers in business, but have no real place in fortune-making that starts from where we are and uses what we have, on which to build real happiness.

Hidden Eoh suggests that you may be wasting energy on unrealistic dreams rather than maximising the many advantages and opportunities you do have. Whatever our age and stage of life, we are bound by some limitations. Even at 17, you have thrown away those teen magazine dreams when boy meets girl in the technicolour world of designer princesses and football millionaires – you realise that the life your mother leads isn't a million miles from your own. Meanwhile, the guys from school have forgotten those debates in which they defended your equal rights down to sharing the washing and, five years on, you launder their muddied sports shirts with no more than a feeble smile.

But it's not that bad, even with no crown on your head and no sports car outside the door. You can choose to be a nuclear physicist, which may involve single-minded effort for many years, or to grow beautiful sunflowers. Once you focus on dreams that are realistic and possible for you, and discard the day dreams, you can, given the limitations of the reality principle, make your future what you will.

DAY 14
Peorth – the gambling cup

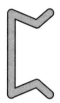

Fate, what is not yet known or revealed, the essential self,
taking a chance

This is perhaps the most important rune and appears when an issue is of relevance to our core self and therefore far more significant that we realised. As such I have devoted more space to it than the other runes.

In the tradition of the early Northern peoples, gambling and divination were very close in function and many decisions would be made by casting – whether to travel or to remain close to home, to fight or to take evasive tactics: the fall of the dice or runes, or whatever was cast, would, it was believed, indicate the will of the gods. 'Testing their luck', first in lot-casting and then in the real world, was a way the Viking warriors discovered truths about their essential self, the root person with both strengths and weakness, vices and virtues, for they did not believe their fate was fixed. The gambler or diviner was expected to read his orlog, or fate, then take appropriate action to either maximise good fortune or avoid any potential pitfalls.

Only the Anglo-Saxon poem mentions Peorth when it speaks of play and laughter in the beer hall among bold men, and so it is essentially a rune of joy.

Rune magic holds a remarkably modern view on our destiny, not as a fate preordained or fixed by powers beyond our consciousness, but as determined by our own actions past and present. The first Norn, or goddess of fate, is called Urdhr and talks of the past, which in the ancient tradition influences not only our own present and future but also that of our descendants. The second Norn, Verdhandi, speaks of present deeds and influences that again are strongly implicated in our future direction. Skuld, the third Norn, talks of what will come to pass, given the intricate web of past and present interaction, and she faces forward, always tearing up and then reforming the old patterns. Our fate, or orlog, is constantly being changed as each new day adds to the web of interaction. The runes were seen as a way of getting to the heart of this intricate maze and so discover potential paths. Any reading containing Peorth has implications for long-term as well as immediate decisions.

Peorth in a reading

Being true to ourselves sounds a strangely old-fashioned concept, but unless we do live by our own basic beliefs and evolve along our unique path, the result may be that we feel alienated and out of touch with others as well as ourselves.

We need to try to connect and remain in touch with the person we are at root; by this I mean the person we were at five years old before life took a hand in mixing the ingredients, the person we shall be when we assume the role of the wise woman imparting wisdom and the benefit of experience to future generations. This distillation of everything that is quintessentially you could be called essence of self. It is Jung's 'inner child', the Fool in the Tarot who has undertaken his quest and gained wisdom – or the you who has recalled and regained the divine knowledge you were born with, that has been diluted on the way through life.

Peorth is the rune that says that it is time to trust our own beliefs and assert our own priorities; this may mean going against the crowd and the advice of others, even those who may be regarded as experts. It is a rune of joy, so rejoice in your unique talents and do not seek to emulate anyone else. Right now, your own special essence will help you to succeed. Trust your own wisdom and if in doubt return to your roots, to the wise child within who can see to the heart of the rainbow if you remove the blinkers of sophistication and doubt placed over your eyes by convention.

Hidden Peorth

When Peorth appears in its hidden aspect, it can suggest that the real person we are at root is being sacrificed to the need to play different roles and fit in with the expectations of others. Women especially can lose contact with their own identity, because others encroach on it and erode it, not least through expectations that we should look and act in certain ways to gain approval.

Hidden Peorth may appear if someone is imposing on you a lifestyle or decision that you do not want, perhaps a house or career move, pressure to have children, to marry or to act in a way that seems wrong to your own deep moral code, even though it may be quite legal and acceptable socially. You may be viewing yourself as you are reflected through the eyes of society or those close to you, and not as you really are. So the vision may be distorted and your view that you are lacking in some way is mistaken. If in doubt, step back and let your essential self speak true, perhaps through Cen, your inner voice and flame.

DAY 15
Eohl – eel-grass

The higher self, spiritual matters, psychic development, the need to take care in a matter of importance; making difficult but necessary decisions

In many ways Eohl is the most difficult rune to understand, for it is given several interpretations, perhaps because there have been different images used to express such a complex concept.

Its Old English name, elk-sedge, means a type of sword. It represents a two-edged blade. Though a double-edged sword may easily injure its user, it is a very powerful weapon with double the power of a conventional blade. The rune shape is taken as a splayed hand held out or the horns of an elk, in another translation, both of which can be used in attack or defence. According to myth, the four sacred elks lived in the World Tree, eating its leaves.

The Anglo-Saxon rune poem interprets it as eel-grass, found on marshes, that grimly wounds anyone who tries to grasp it. Eel-grass has many creative functions. It was used for thatching, kindling for the fire and bedding for animals, once again bringing the notion that anything that is of worth must be handled with care. So too must the path of spiritual growth and divination be approached with respect and not treated as a game or for selfish or negative ends.

If you find this rune hard to interpret in a reading, close your eyes and let images come or words flow.

Eohl in a reading

This is the magic rune that links you with the world of higher states of consciousness, intuition and your own innate psychic and healing powers. It may be cast at a time when you recognise the existence of your innate healing and psychic abilities and may feel close to an angelic guide or your own Higher Self.

You may have become increasingly aware that there is more to life than material success and that for you fulfilment in spiritual matters is becoming a priority. But this does not mean that you have to make a choice between the material world and that of the spirit, for this is a rune of integration. It is not easy to marry the commercial and the spiritual and you will need to use care and great integrity. But women who adopt an altruistic, intuitive approach to their careers seem instinctively to attract good fortune and success that eludes more hard-headed colleagues. Meditation, dream interpretation and creative visualisation are tools of the workshop and boardroom as well as the temple of contemplation. While for some, spirituality involves stepping away from the world, for the majority of women it means meditating on the train. Like their ancestors who saw pictures in the suds of the wash tub and entered mesmeric states as they sat by the bedside of a sick child, for many of today's women the task of incorporating their spiritual nature into their everyday world makes both sides of life richer and more meaningful.

Hidden Eohl

Grasping the nettle, the hidden interpretation of Eohl, is not easy, but once you have made the decision you were avoiding or spoken the difficult words you dreaded saying, you slowly begin to reap the benefits of your courageous action. The fears in the night and the inner rehearsals were all far worse than the moment of truth and you may find that the reality was far less painful than you anticipated. Applying for a job or taking an opportunity that will make great demands of you can be initially daunting. Going out in public for the first time after a relationship has ended or hurtful remarks have shaken your confidence; complaining over an injustice; setting matters straight; apologising; asking for help; making a request; declaring feelings and risking rejection or disapproval: whatever the initial step, it is better to try to act rather than to remain frozen by fear and inactivity (reflections of the Is rune). Years later we may regret not speaking or acting, so take your courage and see what positive results will compensate for the initial pain of firmly grasping the nettle.

DAY 16
Sigil – the sun

Success, ambition – especially in career – energy, expansion, unfulfilled potential, talents, unexpected opportunities that should be seized

As with any divinatory system, the Sun is the most positive and potent symbol, especially in the world of the North where sunshine and warmth were so precious. Sigil can also represent lightning and forms the third and most powerful of the Fire Runes. Solar festivals, especially the longest day or summer solstice, were celebrated throughout the Northern world by great fire-wheels rolled down hills, flaming tar torches carried around the fields and bonfires lit on hilltops to welcome the Sun and give it power.

In the Far North and Scandinavia, the Sun was female. Sol, or Sunna in the Norse tradition, rode her sun chariot drawn by the horses Aarvak (the early waker), and Alavin (the rapid goer), with a golden shield to protect them from the heat of the Sun.

In the Old Norse rune poem Sigil is called 'light of the lands', which refers to its sacred nature as the life-giver, while the Icelandic poem talks of the Sun as the life-long destroyer of Ice, a reminder of how important the Sun was in very cold lands. The Anglo-Saxon poem says that the Sun always brings hope to seafarers. And so this is a rune to be welcomed.

Sigil in a reading

We all have perfect confidence that the sun will rise again and that tomorrow will bring new opportunities or a fresh start and so it would be impossible to find any negative connotations for this rune. Whether it is the dawn of a new day, the power of noon or the fulfilment of effort with the setting sun, the Sun Rune speaks of energy, of growing confidence and of all the talents you have within that are waiting to find expression.

Sigil is about developing those unique gifts that life has given you, now, beginning today, of opening yourself to optimism and belief in your own abilities to succeed in whatever way your dreams direct you. If not now, then in the near future you will be given opportunities to achieve tangible success and joy and you should not let anything stand in your way or allow discouragement from anyone to deter you.

In the *I Ching*, Feng, or Hexagram 55, representing Abundance, the Noonday Sun, is frequently translated as 'Be not sad. Be like the sun at midday.' There cannot always be assurances of permanence in life or love, only the happiness and optimism of the present. To live in the present is to escape the burdens of the past and the need for certainties of the future. So seize the moment and soon joy will be yours.

Hidden Sigil

You may have been offered an opportunity or want to follow a new direction. But all the old voices of doubt linger in your head – remember the embittered aunt who said you were not as pretty as your sister and would never find anyone to love you, the disappointed school teacher who predicted you would never amount to anything, your first lover who pointed out your defects in the finest detail, the employer who told you that you were lucky to have a job at all and had no right to complain that you were expected to work a 12-hour day and then find a late-night shop to buy presents for his wife's birthday that he had forgotten. They are just the voices who had their own agendas and inadequacies to off-load, but they have appeared in several runes and their presence is the single most powerful obstacle to fulfilment.

The Sun Rune is a reminder that you are entitled to your place in the sun. There may be dreams cast aside by other concerns over the years, but Sigil reminds you of your hidden potential and says that there are many dreams you can still fulfil. You may be too old to be a ballet dancer or an airline pilot – you discarded those regrets with Eoh – but your hidden potential, highlighted by the blank aspect of Sigil, can, if released, illuminate every aspect of your life.

A cast of six runes

This is simply two lots of three runes, cast on to your cloth. Wait to interpret the meaning until all six runes have fallen on the cloth. Runes cast later may displace or cover the first ones you threw. As with your cast of three, study the patterns made by the runes, the circles in which they fall and the hidden aspects. As you cast more runes, the empty circles can reveal as much as those containing runes. If, for example, Peorth, the circle of the essential self, is empty, perhaps there is so much happening in your life or the demands of others are so great that you have lost touch with your separate self.

A cast of six can be helpful if you have a more complex question that concerns other people or choices to make.

Jackie's cast of six

Jackie is in her early forties and pregnant for the first time. She and her partner Rick have a very comfortable lifestyle, and enjoy plenty of foreign travel. When they were first married, Rick had said he wouldn't mind a baby some day, but when Jackie didn't become pregnant he refused to go for tests and assumed that they would never have children. Now there is a baby on the way, Rick fears the new arrival will disrupt their lives and he is pressurising Jackie to have an abortion.

Though Jackie greatly enjoys her career as a journalist, she is thrilled at the chance of having a child when she had given up all hope, and feels that, in spite of the changes a baby will bring, it is the next step for her own development. So Jackie does a cast of six, not of course to resolve such a complex and painful issue, but to obtain another standpoint from which she may be able to counter the barrage of logic and persuasion to which she has been subjected by Rick. Jackie also hopes it will help her to get in touch with her own true feelings, which, she admits, are very complex.

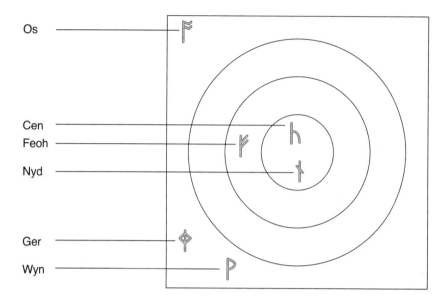

Rune 1: Feoh in Cen, the realm of thoughts and the inner world

Rune 2: Ger, hidden in Is, the realm of what is yet to come

Rune 3: Nyd in Peorth, the circle of the essential self

Rune 4: Os, hidden in Is

Rune 5: Wyn, hidden in Is

Rune 6: Cen in Peorth

Feoh in Cen, circle of thoughts, hopes and fears, represents the price we pay for any decision or action. The high costs to Jackie's own happiness of either going ahead with the baby and accepting a changed life, perhaps without her husband, or giving up the chance of having a baby, are inevitably going round and round in Jackie's thoughts, so making her feel helpless.

Ger, hidden in Is, the rune of the harvest, reflects the feeling that Jackie has of being trapped in a sterile existence. For, as the days progress, she is increasingly convinced that having a baby is the next natural stage of her life. If she goes against what is for many, though by no means all, women, the natural ticking of the biological clock and her desire to have a child, it may ultimately destroy her relationship with her husband. It is the dilemma of those women who, like their mothers and grandmothers, find after years of enjoying fulfilment through career and adult relationships a moment can come when the call of nature to reproduce becomes too strong to ignore.

Nyd, the rune of needs, is right in the centre of Peorth, Jackie's innermost circle of the essential self. She cannot see her own needs clearly right now, but her distress indicates that they are not being met, although they are central to resolving the whole question. What Jackie needs on the deepest level is the approval and support of her husband, who fathered her child, and his protection during pregnancy when she feels vulnerable. It may be that her need to be protected and cared for hasn't been met in the marriage, where she has always acted as an equal but independent partner and even unconsciously mothered her husband. What she wants and needs now must ultimately be a deciding factor, although of course her needs may not coincide with those of her husband.

Nothing is actually happening in Jackie's outer circle of Rad, the circle of action and interaction. Now is the time for sorting out the past and for making plans for the future.

There is a lot of Is around – not surprisingly as Jackie is in a state of shock. When things are really bad, staying put and doing and saying nothing is sometimes no bad course.

Os (communication) is hidden and immobile in Is. Rick and Jackie are not talking about – and certainly not answering – the real question, which is: what basis for the marriage will remain if Jackie has an abortion against her will?

Runes are not about abstract rights and wrongs, but about feelings and needs of real people in real situations in the real world. There are usually no heroes or villains, but men and women of flesh and blood, simply struggling to do their best in sometimes difficult situations – and sometimes getting it wrong.

Hard though it is, Jackie needs to listen to what her husband is saying and, of course, to express her own needs that were hidden in rune 3 (Nyd).

The appearance of Wyn, the rune of personal joy, might seem surprising, but it is saying that for Jackie her personal happiness is now centred on the life growing inside her, an alien concept to Rick and to Jackie, for at one stage they both believed that a child would be the end of personal freedom. But here Jackie is putting her own (and the baby's) happiness above her husband's desire for a life without responsibility and a relationship that remains static. It would seem that Jackie will, if necessary, go it alone rather than give up the chance of motherhood.

Cen, the inner voice, in the circle of Jackie's essential self, says that when all the pain has subsided a little, she has the answer if she will only listen to herself and draw on both her instinctive feelings and her Higher Self (in the form of Peorth and Eohl) who will speak to her and tell her what to do.

Ultimately this advice from within is better than that which a hundred therapists, friends or clairvoyants could offer. The future of the baby is ultimately down to Jackie, for it is growing in her body and no one can make the decision for her whether or not to go ahead with the pregnancy.

It may be that, faced with the choice of losing Jackie, her husband will grow up himself and support his wife in what she decides. Or it may be that he will go off to find a more supportive environment for himself. But if he forces Jackie to give up the baby, then the reality of the relationship may well be destroyed.

The runes don't promise happiness, only the knowledge that you are making the crucial decisions yourself. If you have peace in yourself, you are never alone, however rocky the path.

I did hear from Jackie some years later. She and Rick had separated and she decided to bring up her daughter alone. However, a few months after the birth, she became involved with an old family friend, Neil. Within a year, he moved in with Jackie and soon afterwards Jackie became pregnant again. This time there was no dilemma. The new family is very close. Rick occasionally visits his daughter, but is married to an older woman without children. Jackie works from home and has a flourishing new career specialising in childcare articles.

Tir – the Pole or Lode Star

Justice, altruism, self-sacrifice, following dreams, keeping faith through difficult times

We now move on to the aett of Tir, the spirit warrior and protector of the weak. Tir is the constant pointer in the Northern skies and represents the guiding star that inspires all endeavours. The Pole Star stood at the top of the World Tree and as such is said always to align people to their spiritual as well as physical path. Shamans or magic men and women in the North often focus on the Pole Star for their astral journeyings. Tir (Tyr or Tiw) is the Norse god who symbolically presided over the Germanic General Assembly and over all matters of justice. Tir is also the god of war because justice was sometimes settled by combat or even full-scale battle. It was believed that Odin and Tir would allow only the just cause to win.

In the Norse and Icelandic poems, Tir is called the one-handed god, referring to the sacrifice he made of the most precious strength of a warrior, his sword hand. This he did to bind Fenris Wolf, to save his fellow gods, as he was warned that the wolf would kill his father Odin. In the Anglo-Saxon rune poem, it is the guiding star aspect of Tir that predominates, being described as a special sign, that keeps course well and never fails.

Tir in a reading

In a reading this is a special sign, a star of inspiration and of faith rewarded. Tir is a reassurance that your life is on the right track and that even if the way ahead seems slow or rocky, if you follow your own unique star path, like the shamans, you will reach the star of fulfilment. You should focus on your dream, however small – and some of us have only small dreams to fulfil one by one. You should not let anyone distract you or tell you that you are misguided. This can be especially important if you are evolving spiritually and those around you do not understand.

Equally, if something is of great importance or a matter of principle, especially if you or someone you care for is being treated unfairly, your loyalty and desire for justice will shine through. Although your fight for justice may not win you many friends among those who insist you should not make a fuss, you know that this is not a case for compromise. Compared to you on the campaign trail, Joan of Arc was an amateur.

You may need to make a sacrifice in the near future for a long-term advantage. An opportunity may appear to follow a dream that seems to involve giving up comfort, ease or security and you wonder if it is worthwhile. It may mean giving up evenings to study, working extra hours to improve long-term prospects or giving up a secure way of life for one that has meaning. Perhaps you are on the path to healing or spiritual development, taking the first steps that seem so difficult to fit in with all the other demands of life, but which are like a guiding star. The inbuilt message is that such efforts will bring rich rewards, not immediately but in the months ahead.

Hidden Tir

It may be that you are sacrificing yourself unnecessarily or for an unworthy cause; perhaps you are the one who always ends up acting as a sponge for the family angst or tolerating unjust behaviour at work. Women make sacrifices every day without a second thought. Some are worthwhile: we have all had to care for a sick child or relative, give up an exciting weekend to attend an important but dull family occasion, face disapproval at work because our child is expecting us to watch his performance as third shepherd.

But many sacrifices, due to the selfishness or inefficiency of others, are not so worthwhile. Over the years I have driven so many children to school who have missed the school bus that I could set up my own transport service. As I have frequently washed up after returning from a late-night broadcast because none of my able-bodied family has bothered in my absence, I have remained silent but seethed inwardly and then compensated by eating too much – or developed a migraine. Martyrs' smiles best suit a plaster saint who is not so prone to wrinkles, and this is the rune that appears most in my readings and one I still struggle with.

Other women I have spoken to from all over Europe and the United States identify with this, whether or not they have children, and cite relationships from which they receive far less than they give – with unreasonable employers, inefficient work colleagues and inflexible officials who demand offerings on the altar of their self-importance. The best thing to give up may be your sacrifices for such unworthy causes, thereby releasing time and energy for the positive aspect of Tir, following your own star.

DAY 18
Beorc – the birch tree

*Renewal, healing, physical or spiritual regeneration, fertility,
nature and the environment*

Beorc is the rune of Nerthus, the ancient Nordic Mother, the Earth
Goddess who was worshipped by the Neolithic peoples of
Scandinavia and Denmark. The tradition continued with Frigga,
or Frigg, wife of Odin, who was associated with fertility and
motherhood and was called upon by women in labour.

This rune contains the concept of the cycle of birth, death and
rebirth. The birch was the first tree to re-colonise the land after
the retreat of the ice-cap at the end of the last Ice Age. According
to the old poems, the birch 'puts forth shoots without seeding and
has shining branches to touch with the sky'.

Birch trees were planted in front of a dwelling in the Northern
countries to invoke the protection of the Earth Mother, and the
custom spread to America with the settlers. Beorc, my personal
favourite, is the green rune of Mother Nature and, like Gyfu, is
central to women in its life-giving, healing aspects.

Beorc in a reading

Women wanting to bear an infant welcome this rune as a sign that
the power of the Mother Goddess is with them, but it is so much
more, like restoring rain followed by sunshine that brings a sense
of anticipation that life will be good.

How can there be doubt when the rune of regeneration, of new life and growth and connection with the earth is cast? It may be a time in your life when you need renewal of enthusiasm, energy or fertility, whether in a relationship, for a child or for new ideas and projects. Since the birch tree seeds of itself, within you is the well-spring of inspiration.

If you are tired or dispirited, go out into the natural world – even the smallest urban park has restorative properties. It is not only ageing hippies from the 1960s who hug trees: the greening power calms and connects us with every woman in every place and time who has come to the forests and woodlands to seek the energy to go on, to rebuild and to give creatively to others.

Your natural healing powers will be to the fore, whether you are formally learning one of the myriad healing techniques, spontaneously stroking the brow of a lover or friend to relieve a migraine, instinctively mending quarrels between loved ones or colleagues, or campaigning to save wildlife, forest, clean beaches and unpolluted skies.

Beorc is above all the rune of a creating new life from old, and fresh hope from what is stagnant or abandoned; it restores the wounded ego in a loved one, breathes love into a relationship temporarily soured, and makes a life for you on your terms, perhaps after disappointment. It connects you with the female power base that is rooted in the earth.

Hidden Beorc

But Mother Earth has a darker side that causes floods, drought or whirlwinds. In the continuing cycle of growth and decay, destruction of the old is an integral part. Hidden Beorc represents the dark power of the Mother, the Greek Hecate, the Crone of the Night, the ancient Bone Goddess who took men and gods apart and reformed them in a new way. Shakti-Kali of the Hindu religion, who dances on the corpse of Shiva, the Father God, to restore him to life and to empower the other gods, is but one example of the fierce aspect of the Mother Goddess.

Even hidden, Beorc is still a power rune, but recognises that transformation is the key to joy. This awareness may involve difficult choices, allowing others to make their own mistakes and live their own lives, even if you can see the pitfalls.

Certain aspects of life change naturally. Some women have more children or immerse themselves in mothering because that is a stage of life that is very powerful for them. Other women who, for whatever reason, did not mother their own children may have immersed their creative energies into many other rich soils. For women, the menopause is the ending of physical fertility, but if used for transformation, it can be the beginning of an immensely rich world of spiritual and emotional fertility.

But there comes a time when a woman needs to centre on herself and the age at which she does so may have nothing to do with the menopause or mothering instincts. When, like the birch tree, she seeds of herself, then she can be most fertile in her own life and in her own way through her relationship with others and most importantly with her self – more of this in the rune Ing.

DAY 19
Eh – the horse

Harmony between people or inner and outer worlds, partnerships and friendships, moving house or changing career

Eh is associated with the horse, an animal sacred to the Vikings, especially the horse that carried its rider into battle. It therefore represents a harmonious relationship as typified between a warrior and his horse. The rune, mentioned only in the Anglo-Saxon rune poem, emphasises the joy a horse brings to his rider and how it can make him feel like a prince.

If a warrior was killed in battle, his horse would often be buried with him, and when a much loved horse died it would be given an elaborate burial too. Odin had an eight-footed grey steed, Sleipnir, as he rode into battle. On his teeth Odin had engraved magical runes that his mount might be invulnerable.

Eh in a reading

This is not a time for independent action, but for co-operation, partnerships and for joint ventures or plans. If you have a problem or you are formulating a plan, it is a good time to consult others, whether your friendly financial adviser, your best friend or an impartial ear. As you talk the matter through, the best course forward will become clear and solutions emerge, possibly with the input of others.

Because the horse is associated with movement, this is a natural time for putting into action any anticipated career, house moves or even holiday plans to acknowledge any restlessness that may be making it hard to concentrate or commit. Sometimes even a day or two away from routine restores enthusiasm and if any relationships are jarring, a short break, either alone or with the person, but away from external tensions that cause friction, would be beneficial.

Above all it is a time for balancing different aspects of your life and perhaps adjusting priorities. Exhaustion can be alleviated by having a few early nights and cutting back on activities that are not necessary or no longer give pleasure. A bit of personal spring-cleaning may identify, for example, a regular commitment or visit to a friend or family member that is no longer necessary and is emotionally draining.

Your rune-reading time marks out a space in your life for you alone and there are many ways you can develop your spiritual potential, informally in your own way and through reading books or attending classes: creating mantras or phrases of power that you can repeat while gazing into a candle flame or watching a fountain or water feature can be a good way of focusing your psychic energies. These less tangible aspects of your life can restore balance when pressures are intense and demands great.

Hidden Eh

Balancing life can be akin to juggling, as you try not only to organise the different aspects of work, home, leisure and the all-important but often forgotten self, but also to reconcile the needs of different people and try to keep them all harmonious. Men can sometimes be like stags in the rutting season, competing for the doe. Sons and husbands, fathers and grandfathers, employers, employees and colleagues are all wanting your attention and locking horns, especially in the home situation. Of course the women in your life may be no better – your mother versus his mother, two grandmothers fighting over a grandchild or two colleagues with egos like eggshells.

You may find yourself feeling distinctly disharmonious and having soothed everyone else's troubled feelings, you finally burst into tears yourself or swear incoherently because the fax machine is jammed or you drop the eggs at the supermarket check-out. The unbalanced nature of most women has less to do with their hormones and more with the conflicts caused by trying to maintain the equilibrium of others.

Stop and make time for yourself, even if it is only 20 minutes every day when you do absolutely nothing. Above all, refuse to act as UN peacekeeper for the quarrels of others amongst family, friends and colleagues. You could actually be fuelling the disharmony around you by leaping in with your white flag every time voices are raised. If there is no audience (i.e. you), then family and office backbiting could lose its attraction for the combatants.

DAY 20
Man – humankind

Wisdom, maturity, acceptance of self and others, hidden strengths and talents, issues of ageing and mortality, our lives as part of a wider pattern

Humankind was seen in the ancient world of the North as a reflection of the divinity fulfilling three functions: warrior, farmer and ruler/magician.

In Norse legend the first man and woman were formed from trees, an ash and an elm. Odin gave them the breath of life, Vili imbued them with intelligence and a loving heart, and Ve brought them their natural senses. Aesc, the man, and Embla, the woman, were given Midgard, Middle Earth, as their home and so began the human race.

At the destruction of the existing order at the Final Battle of Ragnarok, their descendants Lif and Lifthrasir sheltered in the World Tree and survived the holocaust to repopulate the new world.

Man says that although individuals may cease to be, they live on in their deeds and their descendants. This rune therefore is a celebration of the strengths and potentials of individuals and their connection to the human race in all times and places, Jung's two-million-year-old man who is said to be within us all. Humankind is formed by the quickening of dust into life, according to the Norse poems. The Anglo-Saxon poem emphasises the mortality aspect and this is one rune where the Christian concepts of the scribes have overridden its original, more joyous meanings (more of this in Ear, the rune of dust).

Man in a reading

Man is a very profound rune and talks of the importance of wisdom and experience. Younger women who select this rune are usually wise beyond their years for it is the rune of the wise counsellor, who can see her own life and those of others as part of a wider canvas. Young or old, you will need to make judgements and counsel others from your own experience, both your own family and people from a wider sphere. You are the sort of woman who finds herself being told the life story and sorrows of the person in the next seat on the train, and even strangers constantly seek you out for advice.

Whatever your age, your inner beauty shines through and you are not a slave to fads of fashion.

Use your natural strengths to the full to create a life that is worthwhile in the way that is right for you, but do not be afraid to admit your own weakness and need for support from others. Because you are so strong and capable, others may not realise when you feel vulnerable, so it is important to ask. Using the Gyfu rune, letting others give to you can empower them and prevent you from becoming drained by the many demands placed upon you for your counsel.

Hidden Man

Most women are brilliant at making allowances for the weaknesses of others and being remarkably honest about their own mistakes. But in doing so, they can underestimate their own strengths and abilities and see others as more competent, organised or happier than themselves.

But if you really listen to them, you may find that they regarded you in the same way: they thought you were Mrs or Ms Unflappable. For Mrs Perfect, that slim, always-smiling hub of the newly laundered family that inhabits the land of television advertisements is just a myth, as is Ms Have-it-all with her shiny sports car, glossy hair, gleaming smile and adoring partner. See her in the morning and she is a snarling harpy, like the rest of us, laddering her tights and losing the car keys.

But you may have recently been subject to unfair criticism, spite or gossip. Those who need to make others feel inadequate are the ones with the real image problem. Scratch the surface and you will find the spiteful little girl who used to trip you up with her skipping rope in the school playground or the boy who dented your new bicycle, because you rode faster than he could. Think of your detractors as children and they will lose the power to make you feel useless. Just as you fought back in playground days, do not allow them to bully you now – only today you can use logic to defeat them.

DAY 21
Lagu – the lake

Birth and beginnings, emotions, following the flow of events, unconscious wisdom and intuition

Lagu is the rune of Water or the sea and the ancient poems tell of the hazards of 'churning water' and the brine stallion that does not heed its bridle. To the Vikings, water was a frightening yet exciting concept: sea journeys could be hazardous, but could lead to wondrous journeys and great conquests and discovery of new lands. In the tales of noble exploits it is forgotten that many did not survive the voyages over stormy oceans.

The Nordic gods and goddesses of the sea both gave and took life and offered fertility and wealth. Sailors would always carry a coin with a hole in it or gold earring so that they might pay a tribute to Ran, sister and consort of Aegir, the principal sea god, so that they might live in her coral caves under the waves if they drowned.

When the leader of an expedition approached a new shore, he would throw into the seas the ainstafar (huge wooden posts from the hall abandoned at home). Where the currents carried the posts ashore the explorers would land and mark out their new territory.

Lagu in a reading

Like Eh, the horse, this is a rune of movement and exploration and may be cast at a time when you desire or are planning to embark on a new beginning. Because it is the rune of Water, Lagu talks about going with the flow, as we used to say in the 1960s, following any avenue that opens, even if at first it does not seem promising. The rune carries the meaning of uncertainty, but in the sense of anticipation and regarding the future as an adventure.

In the Northern and Mediterranean traditions, the element of Water represents emotions and intuition and so at this point you should let your feelings rather than logic or the opinions of others guide your decisions. Emotions are woman's greatest gift, the ability to be moved by the sorrow of others, to share their joys as well as pain, to sympathise with the world and empathise with what others are feeling.

These feelings are very different from sentiment and are closely linked with your natural intuition that so often proves to be the best guide to people and situations. What people say and what they mean may be very different and so you should look beneath the surface. A heart to heart is a popular expression for a meaningful conversation about core issues and to speak from your heart may be the key to happiness and positive communication.

Your new beginning may need to be carried out with great sensitivity, and if you have been hurt or suffered difficulties in any aspect of your life, you should allow your trust and confidence to rebuild slowly. The mightiest river comes from a small spring on a mountainside or plain and so what you initiate now will have great significance in the future.

Hidden Lagu

Emotional manipulation, if not emotional blackmail, is the hidden aspect of Lagu. Emotion and sentiment are very different. Perhaps an ex-lover keeps sending flowers and declarations of love when you know in your heart the relationship was not working or was destructive and that if you were together again, within weeks the old problems would return.

Or you may have an employee who keeps coming to you with one tale of woe after another; they frequently miss work, are invariably late and incompetent and they are losing you business, but if you let them go, no one else will offer them employment and their five children and six cats all with kittens will be on the streets, because of you. Or perhaps your adult children may have returned home yet again and be demanding room service in the cheapest hotel in town or may be pressurising you to babysit constantly for their offspring so that they enjoy their social life.

When we are influenced unduly by other people orchestrating our sentiments, it may be that we are actually perpetuating the situation by removing the need for them to cope. Of course you are not going to leave an ageing relative alone at Christmas nor turn down a neighbour or friend's genuine plea for help, but you can gradually withdraw the level of your support to those who do not need it. A hale and hearty parent does not need your company every weekend because they have offended every other member of the family; a wealthy colleague who always asks for a lift and never contributes towards petrol could take the train – or at the very least make lift-sharing a more attractive option to you. It can be hard to refuse aid especially when you have feelings for the emotional or financial sponge.

If you suspect you are susceptible to this kind of behaviour, listen to your heart and imagine you are advising someone else in the same situation.

DAY 22
Ing – the corn god

*Protection, fertility, withdrawal in order to grow strong, waiting,
allowing events to take their course*

Like Ger and Beorc, Ing is a fertility rune with powerful
associations with the natural world and the harvest. Ing was the
ancient Germanic Earth God, consort of Nerthus. As in many of
the old Earth religions, Ing as Corn God died each year at harvest
time and was reborn at the midwinter solstice to bring new life in
the spring. Ing was traditionally the god of the hearth and the
huge old fireplaces that had seats were called inglenooks because
the members of the household were contained close to the fire. So
it is a protective rune, especially of the home, seen even today
engraved on the outside of gable ends.

Ing's sacred wagon made a circuit of the fields after the winter in a
ritual re-enactment, bringing fertility back to the land. In the
Anglo-Saxon rune poem, the only one to mention him, Ing rides
his wagon eastwards, or backwards as it is sometimes translated,
against the natural progression of the Sun, over the waves. This
journey led to the realm of darkness inhabited by the Etins, or
Giants, and refers to Ing's annual, ritual death at harvest time.

The constellation called Ursa Major, or the Great Bear in Western
astrology, was known in Northern tradition as the Wagon.

Ing in a reading

The message of the Ing rune is that you need to initiate plans for the future and allow them to take root so that they may bear fruit some months ahead. So this is very much a rune of patience, totally at odds with the modern world where everything – food, love and success – has to be instant. Fruit and vegetables are forced ahead of their season by intensive farming methods, but this unnatural interference means that they lack the maturity of growing slowly in the sunshine.

Whether you desire love, a baby, success or promotion, now is the time to set your plan in motion and let a relationship or project evolve slowly through patience and quiet effort, rather than seeking instant results or gratification. Some modern fertility problems occur through anxiety when women stop using the contraceptive pill and find they do not become instantly pregnant. In earlier times, human fertility was inextricably linked with the land and couples would make love in the fields on May Eve and at the summer solstice, so harnessing natural energies.

But more generally Ing talks about the natural rhythms of a woman's life. Some PMT is caused, as I mentioned earlier in the book, by modern women not having the chance to slow down during their personal waning cycle. Whether a women menstruates or is in the next spiritual phase of her fertility, there are times when she needs to slow down and withdraw even for a few hours for gentle exercise, contemplation or sleep. Our cat sisters have perfected the art of pacing themselves.

So switch off the computer, turn on the answering machine for a few minutes each day and gaze at a beautiful flower, sit by flowing water or watch the pictures in the clouds, withdrawing to your still inner core so that your creativity can be restored. If you listen to your body, it will tell you when it needs rest: too often this is taken as a signal that food, alcohol or tobacco are needed, which may give a temporary energy boost, but leave the basic need unanswered. Guard your lunch and coffee breaks jealously – they are not the time to sort out problems or dash round the shops.

Hidden Ing

You have done your best in a particular situation, perhaps tried to make peace but have been rebuffed, or you have worked incredibly hard but seem to have received little recognition for your efforts. Perhaps a love affair did not come to fruition or you have initiated so many projects that you are feeling tired. It may be that you now need to let the situation lie fallow – time really is a great healer and restorer.

Now is the time to withdraw and see only those people who make you feel good about yourself. It is not a time for the input of amateur psychoanalysts or those who want to point out shortcomings 'for your own good'.

If you feel angry or frustrated, cast flowers off a bridge, stones into the water or bury a symbol in your garden and plant the seeds of spring around it. Nurture yourself by doing something small each day for yourself; take a long fragrant bath, watch a sentimental movie, have an hour with a book you do not need to read for work, play Mah Jong or Patience on the computer. Leave the chores and the paperwork until tomorrow.

Odal – the homestead

*Home, domestic matters, friendship, the family and family
finances, stability, responsibility and security*

Odal is the rune of the sacred enclosure, the homeland, the
village, the homestead. It is the rune of the home and family and
the customs, duties and responsibilities that go with them. In the
rune poems, Odal is said to be beloved of every human but this
domestic contentment is linked with a good harvest, i.e. material
comfort. Though the Norse people were great wanderers the
homestead was, nevertheless, important to them and establishing
a new home, however temporary, in a new land was a priority, as
was shown in the rune Lagu.

Odal in a reading

Domestic issues are to the fore, whether you live alone or with
family and friends, whether you are a traveller or have a
permanent dwelling. So it is a time not for high passion and
excitement but for nest-building and maintenance. You may be
leaving home for the first time or considering moving house,
perhaps to a different kind of accommodation if circumstances
have changed. Friends and family are important right now, as is
working to secure your finances, especially if these have been
erratic.

You have the ability to create a welcoming atmosphere for others
and yourself wherever you live and work and this is a gift that
attracts many to you.

Perhaps outside influences have been disrupting your home life, former family members have moved on or new ones joined the family circle, so it is a good time to weave together family unity and sort out issues of priorities and loyalties. With divorce and remarriage being so common nowadays, even a woman who lives alone can have an amazing assortment of single family members, step-relatives and close friends who may have separated. Conflicting loyalties can be a problem, but it is important not to allow warring parties to force you into choices you do not want to make, and to keep peace in your own home at all costs.

At work it is also a time for maintaining the status quo, making do and mending rather than starting again, until you are sufficiently secure financially and emotionally to cast your ainsta far from your ship to establish a base in a new land or workplace. Though progress may seem slow, just one step at a time, you are creating firm foundations for happiness in all aspects of your life, so this is a rune to be welcomed.

Hidden Odal

All is not well at the homestead and financial or practical considerations may seem insurmountable. You may feel threatened by the gathering hordes outside and within. Perhaps at work it is just not possible to do everything that is demanded of you. And when you summon your allies, they are all washing their hair (no doubt using your shampoo) or off hunting in the urban jungle. So you are left to entertain your partner's mother, which involves shopping, cooking, cleaning for a full military inspection, nailing back on the wall the shelf he erected and reinforcing it to hold the vase she sent at Christmas, knowing that tomorrow you will be expected to present the accounts to your company's auditor. 'Poor boy, he works so hard,' the doting mother sighs and you send fond thoughts to the bar stool on which he is propped.

Harmony lies in reorganisation – 'prioritising' as it is currently known – and using your brilliant organisational skills to make your own domestic and world of work easier for you. This may involve a step-by-step process to reprogramme the other characters in your domestic or office soap opera. If money is draining from the home through unnecessary trivial wastage – for example flatmates leaving lights on when the electricity bill is shared – you need to draw up rules and make sure there is a fair division of finances. All this may seem a million miles from the spiritual aspects of the runes, but if you are constantly tired, enervated or resentful, meditation, visualisation and empowerment rituals will fall on stony ground – or you will fall asleep. More practical measures are called for in this situation.

DAY 24
Daeg – the dawn

Sudden clarity after doubt or confusion, enlightenment, light at the end of the tunnel, optimism, a chance to wipe the slate clean

In Norse legend, Nott, the goddess of night, gave birth to a radiant son, Daeg, whose name meant day. As soon as the gods saw the radiance of Daeg they fashioned him a chariot, drawn by a white steed called Skin-faxi (Shining Mane). From its mane, brilliant beams of light radiated in all directions, scattering the fears of night.

Daeg refers to the coming together of day and night at sunset, the beginning of a new day in the Northern world and also at daybreak or dawn. Daeg is therefore the moment of fusion and transition and so has special potency. It is the balancing of opposites and like the World card in the Tarot, the uniting of disparate forces in harmony, synthesis and integration. With this harmony comes the expansion of possibilities and the widening of horizons, physically, mentally and spiritually

The Anglo-Saxon rune poem, the only one to describe Daeg, refers to it as the Lord's messenger. This is another example of Christianity in the rune poems. But whether it is the light of day, of the Sun God or of the Christian Godhead who offers enlightenment, the light of Daeg shines on rich and poor alike, bringing them hope.

Daeg in a reading

This is the 'good fairy' rune. The light is there if we just look hard enough. The cloud hanging over you really does have a silver lining and in the very near future life will begin to make sense and the last piece in the jigsaw puzzle will fit so that you can see the overall shape of the picture. The psychologist Abraham Maslow described peak experiences, those moments of illumination and joy that seem out of time and so intense that life will never be the same. Some women experience these during orgasm with a partner with whom there is spiritual as well as physical connection, others through meditation.

But for most people they are totally spontaneous and unexpected, prompted by a glorious sunrise, small moments of joy, a baby's first smile, the declaration of love when all hope seemed lost, an unexpected kindness, the glorious sensation of staying effortlessly upright for the first time on a bicycle or surfboard.

And so you find that life does get easier and the light gets nearer. You may travel, give accurate and illuminating rune readings to friends and strangers without once thinking about the meanings. You pass the exam, succeed in an interview or just wake up and look at the garden and realise that what you have is what you want, that your relationship or life alone feels right and that you are in control of your destiny.

Hidden Daeg

The good fairy rune cannot have a negative meaning. But daylight may be slower than you hoped in coming and you may wonder if your luck will ever turn and your endeavours come to fruition. Take heart, you are on the right track. The answer is there. Keep faith with yourself and gradually the light will get closer and you will know that it has all been worthwhile.

A circle cast of nine runes

For important issues and for life reviews, a cast of nine runes can reveal a great deal of information through both the positions of the runes relative to one another and the circles that are occupied. You can cast the runes as three sets of three and then read them either in order of casting or the largest cluster first. A cast of nine is most helpful in assessing your own life and so should be carried out every two or three weeks, unless you are experiencing a particularly significant and difficult period, when a weekly review may be helpful. When reading for others, a nine-rune reading is better than a smaller rune cast in building up a picture of underlying issues, especially if the questioner is a stranger to you.

Susanne's cast of nine

Susanne is divorced and in her early fifties. She is the author of a popular series of history books and, now her children have left home, is planning to move to Spain to work as she hates the grey English winter.

But having put her house on the market she has been offered a lecturing post at the local university and the opportunity to work with a research team devising historical workbooks for schools. The post would offer her security, holiday and sickness benefits and a pension scheme, which she does not have at present. Susanne is aware that writing is an uncertain business. But she has loved Spain since she first visited it as a teenager and speaks fluent Spanish. Her dream has always been to live there. Her adult children are trying to persuade Susanne that she should take the safe option.

I have divided the runes into three sets of three, so that you can see the way the reading builds up.

Susanne casts from a full set of runes:

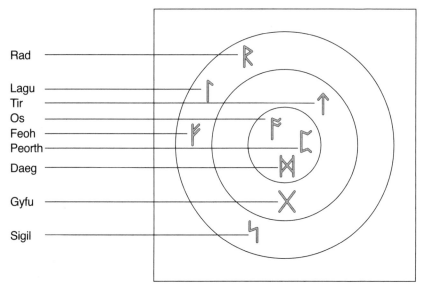

Rune 1: Tir in Cen, the circle of her inner world

Rune 2: Daeg, hidden in Peorth, the circle of her essential self

Rune 3: Sigil, hidden in Rad, the circle of action and interaction

Tir in the circle of Cen says that Susanne is contemplating following her guiding star, which in this case is leading her to Spain. Though her dream is at the planning stage still, it is clearly important and promises fulfilment.

Daeg is hidden in the circle of Peorth and so the light (maybe literally the clear sunlight of Spain) and expansion of horizons are obviously essential to her real person; they may be hidden because Susanne is frustrated that, now the chance to follow her dream has occurred, a safer option on the horizon is creating doubts. This rune says that she must be true to her essential self.

Sigil, the Sun Rune, hidden in Rad, talks of her as yet unfulfilled potential that needs to find fulfilment. One might interpret this as the opportunities in the lecturing and the research job but since Susanne says she loves writing and Spain is a land of the sun Susanne herself regarded this as encouragement that Spain was the right choice for her. What is more, she had been asked by her publisher to write a historical novel based in Spain and had hoped to research the history of Andalucia while living there. It had been Susanne's ambition for years to branch into fiction.

Rune 4: Rad in Rad, the circle of action and interaction

Rune 5: Lagu, also in the circle of Rad

Rune 6: Gyfu, hidden, in Cen, the world of her thoughts

Rad in Rad is definitely an indication of movement, travel and actually fulfilling dreams rather than sitting in those dusty halls like the ancient Vikings, talking about the glorious past and what they would do when the weather improved.

Lagu in Rad is also a rune that a flower child of the 1960s would recognise: it says, 'Follow your heart and go with the flow'. But it also warns that what people say may be different from what they mean to say, a concept that is explained in the next rune.

Gyfu, hidden in Cen, indicates giving after the original need has passed in a relationship. I was unsure, but Susanne identified this instantly as her children, whom she felt guilty about leaving, even though she would only be a two-hour plane journey away. Her 25-year-old daughter, Kate, was working and settled in a relationship and was concerned that her mother should make provision for the future and security. But Susanne's son Josh was the real problem and was extremely vehement that his mother should take the safe option. A perpetual student of 28, Josh still returned home frequently between his ever-changing relationships and whenever his bank manager refused to increase his overdraft. How would he manage? I have met a number of women who are about to spread their wings or embark on a new love affair after years alone, whose adult children become traditionalists overnight and advise caution.

Even modern children like their parents to be predictable, and sometimes, as in Josh's case, there is a hidden agenda. Susanne admitted that Josh had a strong sense of self-preservation and was unlikely to starve, even if she went away. But was Kate right – was Susanne too old to go off gallivanting?

Rune 7: Feoh in Rad, the circle of action and interaction

Rune 8: Os in Peorth, the circle of the essential self

Rune 9: Peorth in Peorth

Feoh, in Rad, is the rune of the price we must pay for any action. Though Susanne was successful in her writing with several future contracts, the real price of not taking the lecturing job was continuing financial uncertainty. The need to sort out her long-term economic future was the central issue, whatever she decided.

Susanne admitted she had been advised by her accountant to put money into a pension and a sickness scheme, but she had never got round to it. Now might be the time while she was earning high royalties. Another option the accountant had suggested was that she rented out her home, at least for the first year, rather than selling it, while she discovered if the reality was as good as the dream. Kate acknowledged that this might be wise.

Os, communication in her circle of essential self, could refer to either option, but it was overlaid by Peorth, the real Susanne in its own realm, an indication that what she was doing, i.e. writing, was what she really wanted to do. Susanne said that from an early age she had always wanted to write. She had worked as a history teacher for some years, but although she was competent, she felt she was fulfilling her late mother's dream, not her own; her mother had persuaded her to train as a teacher as a safe job. But she said she felt no enthusiasm at the idea of preparing teaching materials for schools and the university post would reduce greatly her hours for creative writing.

It can be argued that we interpret the runes according to what we want. Even if that were true, it would be no bad thing, for it would mean we guided ourselves rather than being guided by others. But the fact remains that Susanne selected runes that talk of change and the essential self and not those that speak of safety, learning, nest-building or making do and mending.

I lost touch with Susanne when she moved to Spain, which she did after renting rather than selling her home and setting up insurance policies for health cover and a pension.

DAY 25
Ac – the oak tree

Independence, power, authority, traditional wisdom and learning

These runes make up the aett of Odin the All-father. This is an incomplete rune row that either was added at a later date or in which the other runes have been lost with time.

Just as the birch is the tree of the Earth Goddess, so the oak is the tree of the Sky Father, sacred to Odin and Thor. The Celtic Druids, whose name literally means 'wisdom of the oak', believed that individuals who acquire the wisdom of the oak attain mastery over nature, not least their own. The Anglo-Saxon rune poem, the only one that mentions the oak, praises its usefulness on land and sea. On land, the poem refers to the acorn, the seed of wisdom, and suggests that much time and effort are needed to acquire true wisdom.

Ac in a reading

This rune is the animus or power side of the woman corresponding to the Emperor in the Tarot. It appears in a reading at a time when assertiveness and following convention are the way to success. This means acquiring every possible last drop of expertise in your chosen field or whatever is the current focus of your life. If, for example, you have financial problems, study all the options as you would in an academic subject and make sure you are well versed in financial law so that you can obtain the best deal for yourself. If you are ill or have legal problems, find out everything you can about your rights and about alternative approaches, so that you are not overwhelmed by the expertise of others who may not always give the best advice for you.

Ac, the tree of independence, may appear when you are contemplating striking out alone, in a business venture, or a personal capacity, or strengthening your identity within a relationship or situation where you have perhaps been too compliant. Peorth, the rune of the essential self, may also be cast in the reading. Make sure you back up your opinions with fact and logic, for this is the rune of using the head rather than the heart.

You may find yourself called upon to take the lead, perhaps over a matter about which you feel strongly. Trust in your own abilities and do not be afraid to speak out. Remember that assertiveness and aggression are very different – it was in channelling the power of the storm that the Druids obtained mastery. If you can respond to any challenge calmly and yet with authority, you can take control of the situation and achieve your goal.

Hidden Ac

You may have been suffering from one too many authority figures and experts in your life recently – it may be an officious teacher who insists she has learned more about your child after half a term than you have in a lifetime, a medical adviser who is insisting on a specific course of treatment for you or a loved one and refuses to discuss options, a bureaucrat who dogmatically enforces every letter of the by-laws, an autocratic neighbour who complains that your growing wild flowers instead of neat borders in your garden is lowering the tone of the neighbourhood. If you do feel undermined or threatened, find yourself an oak tree and let its power and confidence flow through you. Then muster your facts and figures and go forth to battle. Believe in yourself and use logic to defeat bullying. This rune links strongly with hidden Aesc, with which it frequently appears in readings.

DAY 26
Aesc – the ash tree

Spiritual potential, strength, determination and resistance to opposition, endurance, health and healing

Ash is another Father Tree, the tree of the world axis, Yggdrassil, sacred to Odin in his role of wise father and defender. It is the tree of the traveller, in the realms of wisdom by the Father Gods, in the expansion of spiritual potential or in the exploration of far-off lands. In the Anglo-Saxon rune poem, the only one to mention Aesc, the ash looms high and stands firm against many foes.

And so the strength and the resilience of the ash make this a powerful rune to cast in any situation that challenges you or lingers on, wearing down your resistance.

Aesc in a reading

The strength of Aesc can appear when a woman is fighting her way to success, in spite of opposition. Ten years after I first started writing about the runes, the invisible but impenetrable glass ceiling still exists in some areas for women. Equality laws in the UK have improved women's rights in the workplace, but throughout the world there are still hidden obstacles for women.

When Helena, a successful businesswoman in Sweden, a land of equal opportunity, went to visit her bank manager to discuss plans for expansion of her firm, she was asked what her husband thought. Helena received a relatively small loan, because the bank official was worried that she might fall pregnant. She finds that only by using a male accountant is her work taken seriously. In spite of this, Helena's business goes from strength to strength, though she often does her bookwork at home after her family are asleep. Women tend not to compartmentalise: the female workaholic works hard in every aspect of her life.

The power of Aesc resides in whatever area of life forms the focus of your determination. It is the innate ability to overcome all difficulties by sheer perseverance, whatever the obstacles to success, love or happiness, whether physical or more subtle.

The rune also talks about achieving spiritual strength and mastery, especially in the healing arts, astral protection and work with the aura, for the ash is traditionally the tree of healing and one that looms high. Such spiritual growth is all the more potent because you may have to strive hard to make the time and space to meditate, to learn divination or to give yourself space so that your inner world may evolve through dreams and daytime visions. Those who have the time and money to devote their lives to finding spiritual fulfilment sometimes lack the clarity and focus of women who can only find time to listen to tapes on esoteric wisdom on the train or bus, and concentrate their energies in the spare minutes after the day has wound down.

Hidden Aesc

Strength and endurance may be fine words, but if you are caring for an elderly or sick relative or small children with little support, cannot find a job no matter how hard you try or are yourself suffering from a debilitating illness, you may wonder if life will ever improve or how you have the strength to go on. Whatever the challenges in your life, it is important to safeguard your own health, resting at every opportunity, eating well and avoiding stressful situations whenever possible.

As this is a rune that counsels patience, hidden Aesc may appear if you are still young and faced with seemingly impossible targets such as waiting to get through a course, or finding a roof over your head. The ash rune promises that whether you are setting out in life, looking for work or qualifications or are more mature and hemmed in by circumstance, the present situation won't last forever, so don't give up hope. Perhaps you can make small improvements or plans to get ready for the time when you are able to make changes. If you are ill, disabled or depressed, persevere through the medical and therapeutic jungle to get the help or second opinion you need – not easy if you are feeling vulnerable. Try to find support from a sympathetic, practical listener.

DAY 27
Yr – the bow

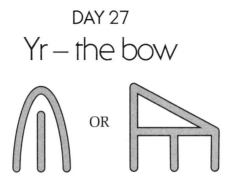

OR

Inner resources, transformation, rebuilding and focusing on goals

In the Anglo-Saxon poem, the bow is said to be a joy to princes and nobles and quick to its course. Made from the yew tree, the tree of endings and also of immortality, Yr bears the Viking name for the rune of the yew tree itself. But in the Anglo-Saxon system Yr is the tree transformed to a weapon, not only for fighting, but for hunting. So from destruction and finality come transformation, life and purpose. The rune of the bow and the rune of the yew tree often appear together, usually after a setback.

Yr in a reading

Yr says that whatever has happened in your life is of value, as long as you can pluck away the dead wood and see the new growth beneath. It is also the rune of clear focus, of aiming for your target in life and concentrating single-mindedly for now on the short-term goal. Women who fit a thousand and one things in their lives sometimes find this difficult but, for the immediate future, one aspect of your life needs to take priority. Once you have attained your goal, you can then integrate once more the other areas that were temporarily set aside.

This rune may appear when there is a sudden urgent need or desire, perhaps a particular relationship that has reached a crucial stage, an impending examination, test or interview, a particular piece of work that must be completed or even a family member or friend who needs attention. Or you may feel that you have an important decision and urgently need time and space to work though the options. Though it may seem that there is no way you can find the time right now, reorganise, delegate, do less than normal in other less pressing areas of your life and then you can concentrate single-mindedly.

Hidden Yr

If Yr is hidden in a reading, perhaps you are clinging to a redundant stage in your life that is far more restrictive than you realise. Or you may have experienced a loss of confidence, problems at work, a betrayal or the ending of a relationship, a decline in health or financial problems; or perhaps you are suffering the consequences of a setback for someone you love.

You may feel that you cannot start all over again from scratch. But you are not starting from nothing. Whatever your age, your experiences, even negative ones, have made you wise, more compassionate. You are less easily swayed by the criticism or fickleness of others. Life will not be the same, but neither are you and you can, given courage, fashion for yourself a new world, taking from the past what is of use. More of this in Ear, the rune of dust.

Iar – the beaver

Adaptability, versatility, maximum effort, the ability to integrate all aspects of life and self

Iar reflects the Viking soul: adaptable to any circumstance, willing to give its all, whatever the odds. In the Anglo-Saxon rune poem, the beaver is seen to live happily, ranging on land for food, but with a dwelling lapped round by water. After the strength of the Father Trees and the focus of the bow comes versatility, the quality that enabled the Vikings to settle wherever they landed, from the icy wastes of Greenland to Greece and Africa. And today, this rune may mediate in many difficult situations where force or capitulation would be equally unproductive.

Iar in a reading

Making the best of things, turning disaster to triumph, is the quality that is one of woman's greatest strengths. On the most mundane level when an outing or holiday is threatened by rain, sub-standard transport or poor accommodation and all about her are complaining, blaming or becoming depressed, the average female will in a trice make alternative arrangements, transform a rain-sodden picnic into a warming feast and manage to make the guys think it was all their idea.

On a more serious level, some women will accept less than ideal careers because the hours fit in with their other commitments, will create a mini-industry out of a hobby to solve a financial crisis, take a second-choice college place and succeed far better than they might have done on the original course, and work on an ailing relationship to breathe new life into it. Statistically, far fewer women than men walk away from commitments on the strength of promises of instant happiness and fulfilment.

You may be facing a compromise or perhaps you are being forced to adapt your dreams and work within limitations imposed by others. Because Iar is also the rune of hard work and input, you may find yourself giving far more than you are receiving. The choice may be between giving a situation your all in the hope of attaining 50 per cent of your dream, or not trying at all. Extra input now will bear fruit in the future – look out for Ger, the harvest, in your reading and keep the ultimate goal open-ended (it may be even better than the one you anticipated).

Hidden Iar

It can be quite daunting to try something different: it may be new technology at work, or a physical skill you hated at school, but now need. Take, for example, my own fear of swimming that I had to try to overcome when I had children; I am still an apprehensive water baby, but all my children are strong swimmers.

You may need to change the opinions and attitudes that you have held from childhood to adapt to your current situation or relationships. How often have we said, 'I would never do that/say that, even if my life depended on it'. But you may be forced to work for an organisation whose principles and mode of operating you dislike, or you may have to develop a career in a field that was dictated by necessity rather than choice. You may find that your children's friends or lifestyle are not what you would have chosen. You may fall in love with a guy who keeps snakes in the bath or plays football three times a week, and because it is difficult to change what a person is without losing the essential person you love, you need to decide how far in any situation you can compromise without sacrificing your own core self, and whether to adapt or walk away.

So this is a rune to take time reading, as choices may be crucial.

Ear – dust

*Recognition that things may outgrow their usefulness; also
integration, a return to optimism, now tempered by understanding*

This is the most woeful of the runes and in the Anglo-Saxon rune
poem is spoken of as fruits falling, joys passing away and
covenants failing. Of course, the poem has been Christianised and
since man was made of the dust of the earth, Ear does contain the
potential for new life. What is missing right now is the creative
spark that is not there or has left the creation. And as humankind
was created from the dust of the earth and returns to it in death, so
the cycles of nature, regeneration and renewal will follow, as
spring follows winter and day succeeds night.

The marked face of Ear and the hidden side are different only in
degree and so, unlike the other runes, both contain the seeds of
sterility and potential future fertility.

Ear and hidden Ear in a reading

Ear reflects a state that is or has been in the past and has not been
resolved in your mind. It does not predict death, relationships or
careers turning to dust. We must realise that if avenues did not
close, we would not evolve personally or professionally and
certainly not spiritually. This rune is linked closely with the blank
rune, the Destiny Rune, the future you have yet to make, and on
page 119 I have included a ritual that marks the transformation
symbolically from dust to destiny.

It is painful to acknowledge that a particular relationship or friendship or a stage in a relationship has run its course or is not going to develop in the way you hoped. The job that was going to lead to a dazzling career may have landed you in a backwater with no chance of advancement; a course of study is not proving as valuable as promised or a particular spiritual teacher is not taking you in the direction you seek to evolve. It may be that you followed a path out of love or to please someone else and you realise it is not for you. If you have the powerful oak, the persistent ash or the adaptable beaver rune also in your reading, it may be time to try another avenue of approach.

Fate is not forcing you to abandon your dreams, but you may choose to consign a particular situation or experience to dust and allow Mother Earth in her own time to transform the experience as part of your inner growth and path to wisdom. The choice must be yours: no one, rune mistress or therapist with a consulting room wall filled with diplomas, has the right to take over that destiny. The runes, like any other divinatory form, are your servants, not your judge.

DAY 30
The blank rune

This is in a sense the first and last rune of any system and the thirtieth in the Anglo-Saxon rune set.

Historically the blank rune cannot be traced back to the early runic systems and so its origins are uncertain. Nevertheless it can be the most important rune in a reading, especially if there is a major decision to make.

It represents the stone of Odin, or the Wyrd (the Fate stone). It is the rune of your destiny and is therefore blank, since you have not yet made that destiny. Who writes on that rune is your choice, although it may not feel so. The blank rune says that you cannot rely on traditional answers, or the advice of others, and that the right course may represent a leap into the unknown. Like the Fool card in the Tarot, it is the rune of intuition and so is potentially very exciting.

Women especially may with the best of motives allow others to write on their blank rune. Years later they may realise that they are living in a way that, although they are not unhappy, nevertheless feels as though they are watching themselves acting a part in a play or moving automatically in a dance; suddenly the words that they want to speak and the path they want to tread become clear.

Transforming the rune of dust to the rune of destiny

✤ Light a small, dark-green, beeswax candle behind your Ear rune and a large creamy-coloured beeswax one behind the blank rune.

✤ Place both candles on a fireproof tray to catch the wax.

✤ When the dark green candle is burned down, etch in the cooling wax with a pin or knife a symbol or letter to represent what is redundant in your life.

✛ Carve over the symbol a large Ear rune and across them both a horizontal cross, the kind marked on hot cross buns, as a symbol of the Earth Mother and regeneration.

✛ Cut out a square of wax containing the symbols and bury it, planting over it lavender for reconciliation of what cannot be. By using pure beeswax you will not harm the earth.

✛ Leave your creamy-white candle burning until sufficient wax has formed to make a circle. Cut this out to form a rune of wax, but do not mark it in any way, as you have yet to make your destiny.

✛ Press small, clear crystal quartz or clear glass nuggets all over the wax circle and leave it in the sunlight and moonlight from the New to the Full Moon, thereafter keeping it wrapped in white silk in a drawer, with rose petals for happiness and love.

✛ Blow or snuff out the candle and make a wish, sending light to all who need it, not forgetting yourself.

✛ You can use the remains of this candle for domestic use, as it is charged with such positive energies.

Empowerments and rituals using your divinatory runes

Ancient rune magic involved complex rituals and was sometimes used for destructive purposes as well as for positive empowerment.

In modern magic, it is recognised that 'hexing', or wishing ill, even to those who wish to harm us, would rebound threefold on the sender. Therefore protective magic has taken the place of more negative forms of defence. Rune magic too has become simpler, as perhaps it always was at root, when practised around the family hearth, rather than in more formal ceremonies.

Each rune relates to a particular area of need and offers a focus and can be used for rituals for love, health, happiness, prosperity, power and success. Modern runic magic concentrates our own inner energies and invokes the divus, the divine or spiritual power within us all, rather than calling upon external deities, though their names are still sometimes used symbolically in ritual.

Using rune magic

I have suggested a simple spell for each rune, based on traditional magical principles from the Northern tradition. For now, you may find it helpful just to read through the general notes that I have given below on the magic of each rune. Then you may use them as a reference list for the days and weeks ahead. Many are connected with the natural world and all you will need is a supply of candles, crystals and a few basic incenses and essential oils that are widely available. You may like to keep a separate box for your magical tools and substances, not because they assume any occult significance, but to mark them as separate from your everyday world. Setting aside a special area of your life is a vital first step towards reclaiming your spirituality.

Feoh magic
Feoh symbolises money matters and is a focus for rituals concerning money-spinning schemes or to resolve financial problems.

Ur magic
Ur rituals offer pure, instinctual power to overcome any obstacles in your path.

Thorn magic
Thorn runes were often carved into buildings for protection. This rune offers protection either as an amulet or in a ritual.

Os magic
Your Os rune can be used when clear communication is needed or you need inspiration for a creative project.

Rad magic
Use Rad spells for instigating change and for travel of all kinds.

Cen magic
Use your Cen rune to get in touch with your inner wisdom when conflicting advice is flying about, or to discover the truth if people are being less than honest or keeping secrets from you that affect your happiness.

Gyfu magic
Gyfu magic is for love, relationships and sexuality between committed lovers.

Wyn magic
You may use your Wyn rune for magic to increase your personal happiness.

Haegl magic
Use your Haegl rune for magic for change under difficult circumstances or if you expect opposition to a new project.

Nyd magic
Use your Nyd rune for magic if you feel neglected or unloved.

Is magic
Use Is magic for preparing for future action and melting away sorrow.

Ger magic
Use your Ger rune for breaking free from a particular path or problems in your life that stop you going forward.

Eoh magic
Eoh magic can help to close a door or mark the end of a phase to clear the way for a new beginning.

Peorth magic
Use your Peorth rune whenever your basic beliefs or identity are under attack or being eroded.

Eohl magic
Use Eohl magic for connecting with your spiritual side and your inner world.

Sigil magic
Use Sigil magic to uncover your hidden talents and potential.

Tir magic
Tir magic helps to focus on long-term gain rather than instant satisfaction.

Beorc magic
Beorc magic is good for regeneration and for fertility.

Eh magic
Use Eh magic when you are feeling fraught or people are criticising you unfairly, especially those in some form of partnership with you.

Man magic
Use the rune of Man to maximise your strengths and let the world see your capabilities.

Lagu magic
Use your Lagu rune for any matter of the heart or your emotions.

Ing magic
Use your Ing rune to restore your inner strength when the world gets too much to bear.

Odal magic
Odal magic can be used for any matters concerning your home or the practical organisation of your life.

Daeg magic
Use your Daeg rune to bring joy into your world.

Ac magic
Use Ac, the rune of the oak tree, sacred to Odin and Thor, when you need to stand apart from the crowd or assert your independence.

Aesc magic
Use Aesc, the World Tree, for perseverance and for healing spells.

Yr magic
Use your Yr, rune of the yew bow, to start again after disappointment or loss.

Iar magic
Use your Iar rune to find a way around difficulties and to adapt your plans rather than giving up.

Ear magic
Use your Ear, rune of dust, to restore purpose and confidence to your life when a person or situation has eroded your belief in your own worth.

Rune spells using the aett of Freyja

A Feoh candle spell for increased wealth

The New Moon period, when the crescent first appears in the sky, and dawn are good times for increasing the flow of money and attracting prosperity.

Because money is associated with the ancient Earth element, take your Feoh rune to a sheltered spot in the garden, a park or open space. Take a gold-coloured coin or a credit card and place it beneath your Feoh rune on a large flat rock or piece of wood. Gold is the colour associated with prosperity.

‡ Light a circle of small golden candles around the rock and visualise golden coins showering upon your Feoh rune.

‡ Lay out a path of flat stones around your rune, encircling the candles and as you step on each stone recite the word 'Feoh', rehearsing in your mind the actual steps you will take to get the money you need.

‡ If you do not force the images, a creative solution may emerge spontaneously as you tread your Feoh path, but if not it will follow in a dream over the next few days.

‡ Take the last stone you step on and, using a paper knife or another stone, etch the runic symbol for prosperity on it.

+ Blow out the candles, visualising the money energies flying into the cosmos, and bury the Feoh stone in the ground near the centre of your candle circle, and plant a golden-blooming herb or flower on top as a sign of your increasing fortune.

+ As the flower grows, it will remind you of your own progress towards your goal.

+ If you prefer, place buttercups, a symbol of riches, or another yellow flower, in a tiny vase on the spot and replace them regularly until you have achieved your aim.

+ Finally, go out into the real world and take the first step, however small, towards making your fortune or solving your financial difficulties.

An Ur weather spell for overcoming difficulties

Wait for a rainy or stormy day when you can utilise the unbridled powers of Nature. Open your windows wide or go out and brave the elements.

+ Write the Ur symbol in red ink or washable marker on a stone, and bind it with red thread or cord.

+ Make a knot for each of the obstacles that face you or ties that hold you back from achieving what you want.

+ Concentrate on each one and as you tie the knot feel yourself fighting against the imprisonment and moving towards what it is you want to be or achieve. Repeat for each knot:

> *Tangle the bonds that me ensnare,*
> *Make me free by the power of Air.*

+ Hold the rune high so that it is exposed to the forces of rain and call its name – 'Ur' – like a wild bull's roar.

* Let the rain blur the symbol, knowing in your heart that that as the stone endures even if the markings wash away, so your innate power to survive and thrive cannot be destroyed by circumstances.

* Cut the knots with a sharp knife or scissors and as the thread falls away, feel your energies welling up inside, breaking the bonds that hold you back.

* Run free through the rain and know that you are no longer the prisoner of others' demands or your own doubts.

A Thorn ritual for deflecting or banishing negative influences and hostility

At dusk, take your Thorn rune for banishing power in your left hand, using your right-brain intuitive powers.

* Place a large red candle behind you so that your outline is reflected in its light.

* Stand in front of a mirror and, with the rune, draw an enclosing sphere around your shape in a single unbroken movement in the air, about 5 cm (2 in) away from your body.

* Visualise the sphere protected by blazing Thorn runes, the diagonals extending outwards to repel physical, psychological or psychic attack.

* Gradually watch the runes fading and as they do so, create a personal signal so that you can reactivate the protection whenever you need it. For example, you might say:

Whenever I trace the Thorn symbol on the palm of my hand or touch my Thorn amulet, the protection of Thorn will surround me and repel all harm.

✢ At night, if you feel vulnerable, etch the Thorn rune on a red candle with an awl or nail, beginning about 2.5 cm (1 in) from the top.

✢ Light the red candle facing your bed and, in your mind's eye, recreate your circle of blazing runes surrounding you.

✢ When the rune is consumed by the flame, blow out the candle and send the protective light to whoever needs it.

An Os water spell to mend a broken friendship or relationship

This is another early morning spell to be used when energies are rising with the new light.

✢ Make an Os rune from a stone and take it to the sea, a lake, river or pond. The Water element is associated with emotions and love.

✢ Place the rune on a flat rock close to the waterside and beneath it place a small photograph or token associated with the estranged person with whom you wish to restore communication.

✢ Surround the rock with small blue flowers such as forget-me-nots (the colour blue is associated with fidelity), or pink flowers, symbolising gentle love and friendship.

✢ Write or scratch the Os symbol on a stick or piece of wood and place this on the water as a symbolic bridge or boat to breach the gap.

✢ Take your flowers one by one and cast them on the water, speaking for each words of love, regret and healing.

✢ Take the Os rune you made and chanting 'Os' softly, circle the photograph or love token nine times clockwise and cast the rune into the water after the flowers.

✧ Wrap the token or picture in white silk with a single red rose and keep it in your drawer until love returns.

After the ritual, make some positive attempt to communicate with your former friend, family member or lover in a non-confrontational way; send a letter, or a postcard of a shared favourite spot, or a small bunch of flowers of the kind you used in the ritual; make a telephone call or visit them. If your efforts are rejected, at least you have tried and can move on with your life.

A Rad noonday spell for a desired journey or holiday

The more detail you can inject into this spell, the more focused it will become. So collect symbols of the journey, for example a toy plane for air travel, a flag of the country you desire to see, a postcard or picture of the specific resort, even a description of the hotel cut from a brochure.

✧ Place all your symbols in a yellow purse, drawstring bag or cloth pocket and finally add your Rad rune.

✧ Wait until the sun is high in the sky and draw an eight-spoked wheel on white paper with a Rad symbol etched in the middle in red.

✧ Mark in the directions with north at the 12 o'clock position. You can use a compass if you wish to align your circle.

✧ In the north of the circle, place a ceramic dish of sea salt for the Earth element; light a sandalwood incense stick in the east for the Air element and an orange candle in a broad candle holder the south of the circle for the Fire element; finally in the west set a glass or crystal dish of water that has been left in the sun- and moonlight for a full 24-hour cycle, for the Water element.

✢ Beginning in the north, sprinkle a few grains of salt over your yellow bag, saying:

Rad, Rad, I call on your energies by the power of Earth and Mother Nerthus.

✢ Pass your bag slowly next through the north-east quadrant to the east and circle it nine times clockwise with your incense stick, forming nine complete smoke circles, saying:

Rad, Rad, I call on your energies by the power of Air and the guiding light of Tir, the Spirit Warrior.

✢ Moving through the south-east quadrant, hold your bag in the south and circle it nine times with the orange candle, saying:

Rad, Rad, I call on your energies by the Power of Fire and of Thor of the Thunder and his mighty hammer.

✢ Moving through the south-west, hold your bag over the west and sprinkle on it a few drops of water, saying as you do so,

Rad, Rad, make swift my journey by the power of Water and of Ran, Goddess of the Waves.

✢ When you have completed the circle by passing your bag through the north-west quadrant to the north, return the yellow bag to the centre of the wheel.

✢ Close your eyes, visualise making your journey step by step in your mind's eye and then snuff out the incense and blow out the candle, using the energies to transport you wherever you wish to go.

✢ Leave your yellow bag near an open window or in the open air until dusk and then place it near your bed so that you may dream of your journey.

A Cen divinatory ritual for a choice between two options that are not clear-cut

✛ Go to a pine wood, in the late afternoon, preferably on a day when the wind is blowing through the trees, so that you can hear its messages.

✛ Cut 12 evenly sized pine twigs, the tree of Cen, from a fallen branch found on the forest floor or taken from a dead tree.

✛ On one side of each twig, etch a Cen symbol, as you do so reciting over and over again a mesmeric mantra, such as:

Cen, torch of brightest fire, show to me my heart's desire.

✛ Tie the twigs loosely into a bundle with scarlet twine.

✛ Place a white unmarked cloth in a clearing encircled by pines, and secure the corners with large pine cones.

✛ Designate one option as the Cen face of the stave. If the issue demands one of two responses, such as yes/no, go/stay, act/wait, attribute the affirmative or active response to Cen.

✛ Stand facing north and shake your bundle of Cen staves over the cloth, so that they scatter.

✛ If any fall off the cloth, disregard them.

✛ If there are more Cens than blank faces or vice versa, then the choice is clear. (If there is an equal number of each, leave the reading for another day.)

✛ Note the answer and remove a stave, retie the bundle and continue the process until you have only one stave left. After each cast, note down the number of Cens.

✛ After the final cast, see whether you cast more Cens or blank answers. If every Cen had been cast in all 11 readings, you would have cast in total 77 Cens.

+ When you return home, light a small, pine-scented candle and arrange your staves in a circle around your divinatory Cen rune.

+ Set the candle within the circle directly behind it. Leave the candle to burn down in a safe place and formulate in your mind the steps you will take to implement your decision.

A Gyfu love spell for consummating love

+ Hang a Gyfu cross, bound with red twine, on the wall at each of the four main compass points about your bed; if possible one branch should be made from ash, a male tree of the Sun, and the other of willow, the female tree of the Moon. Alternatively, you could use oak and rowan, apple and pear, maple and hazel, which are all pairs of male and female trees, but any wood will do. The love ritual works as well between two women, still using the animus/anima polarities so that there is an integration of energies.

+ Place a table at the foot of the bed within the Gyfu branches to hold the ritual objects you will need.

+ Sit on the bed facing your partner and ask them to mark your forehead, breasts and stomach with Gyfu symbols using lipstick or a red body paint, as you chant:

Gyfu in fidelity, two souls entwined in harmony.

+ Take a glass or metal goblet filled with wine and offer it to your partner, saying:

I offer you my body freely, I offer you my mind, my soul, in sickness and health, dearth and wealth, so long as love itself endures.

✛ After your partner has drunk wine from the goblet, lift the cup to your own lips and sit holding it between your cupped hands.

✛ Your partner should then take either an ornamental knife or a wand of ash and gently touch each of the Gyfu runes on your body in turn, beginning first with the forehead, then the left breast, then the right, and finally the stomach, and then plunge the wand into the goblet to symbolise the sacred marriage between Odin and Frigga.

✛ He or she should then mark the surface of the wine with a Gyfu cross, saying:

I offer you protection, I offer you my strength, in sickness and health, dearth and wealth, so long as love itself endures.

✛ Leave the knife in the goblet, place them both on the table and make love.

A Wyn spell to fulfil a secret ambition

✛ On a piece of paper, without conscious thought, write your secret ambition or an unfulfilled dream. You may be surprised at the emergence of a secret ambition that you had forgotten or dismissed as impractical or 'not you'. It may be a modest aim, such as trying a new sport or activity, taking an Advanced Driving Test, or spending a weekend following an interest that you know your friends and family would hate. On the other hand, it may be something much more grandiose, such as getting your book published, moving into the country or across the globe, taking an degree in engineering or archaeology or opening an animal sanctuary. Whatever it is, remember that successful life makeovers can begin in modest ways.

✛ Surround your wish with an unbroken circle of entwined Wyn symbols (the Vikings used these to accumulate power).

✢ Take a helium balloon, if possible decorated with a symbol of what it is you want, for example, a boat for learning to sail or for travelling overseas or a picture of a child if you wanted to become a teacher or have another baby, perhaps late in life.

✢ Tie the paper to the balloon string with nine red knots, and say:

> *Wyn of joy,*
> *Knot of one,*
> *May your power*
> *Into me come.*
> *In Knot of Two,*
> *My wish come true.*
> *Knot of three, knot of four*
> *Upon me abundance pour.*
> *Wyn of joy, in five and six,*
> *My fate is free, my path not fixed.*
> *Knot of seven, knot of eight,*
> *Wyn of joy, let me not wait.*
> *Wyn of Joy,*
> *Complete in Nine,*
> *With this knot*
> *I Luck entwine.*

✢ Take your balloon to the top of a hill or into an open space and, repeating your rhyme with increasing intensity, let the balloon tug faster and faster in the wind, until it breaks free. Alternatively, use a cheap paper kite and tie your wishes to the string. If your balloon goes straight up, you will fulfil your ambition quickly, but however it flies, the Wyn power has been released to help you achieve what you want.

Rune spells using the aett of Haegl

A Haegl egg spell to initiate a plan or decision

+ Take a white egg and make a pin hole in each end, one slightly larger than the other. Shake the egg vigorously, with your fingers over the holes, then blow the contents out through the larger hole, leaving the shell intact.

+ Carefully split the eggshell in half and in one half place a spherical mother of pearl or moonstone with Haegl painted on it in blue to represent the cosmic seed, then close the shell.

+ Surround your shell with six tiny, pink, yellow and pale blue candles, two of each colour, to symbolise the spring and new growth, saying as you light each one:

Haegel take seed, new life bring forth.

+ When the candles are burned through, open the egg and take out the crystal.

+ Sprinkle salt over it for the nourishment of the Earth, pass a musk or pine incense over it for the courage of Air.

+ Finally cast your moonstone into the sea on the turning tide on the seventh wave, or into any running water, saying:

Hail to water, water to sea, seed of life grow strong in me.

+ This is also a good ritual if you want to become pregnant.

A Nyd Fire spell to bring warmth and vitality into your life

✛ Take your Nyd rune into the noonday sun and place it where it can absorb the warmth.

✛ On a long, thin piece of yellow paper, write what you need to make yourself feel happy again. Draw a circle of Nyd runes joined together in a pattern around your words.

✛ On two sticks of wood, draw or etch a Nyd rune.

✛ In a fireproof container or small pit, ignite a small fire, placing the two Nyd twigs in a cross and igniting those first. Alternatively, place them on a lighted barbecue, saying as you do so:

*Nyd, warm my heart, warm my soul, warm my mind that
I may burn with life.*

✛ Cast your paper into the fire and recite your needs.

✛ Sit in the sunshine for a while holding your Nyd rune in your power hand (the one you write with) and let the golden warmth of Fire and Sun enter you.

✛ Let the fire burn out and when you have ensured everything is safe, return home.

✛ Gaze into a mirror with the sunlight behind you or, if it has faded, light a scarlet Fire candle and see your aura flaming golden that reflects not only the light surrounding you but the fire rekindling within.

An Is spell to melt the ice around your heart after a betrayal in love

+ During the period of the Waning Moon, take a natural block of ice or one from a from a refrigerator or freezer and carve in it the Is symbol.

+ Place the ice in a fireproof container to catch the water as it melts.

+ On a green candle, the colour of new growth in nature, etch with an awl or nail the Sigil rune, symbol of the Sun or Fire.

+ Light the candle, chanting softly:

Melt Is and let life flow,

and let the candle flame stand close enough to the ice until it slowly melts.

+ Spend the time it takes the ice to melt throwing away all the old mementoes, letters and tokens associated with the betrayer.

+ Take the water into the garden or to a window box and let it cascade on to plants or flowers, if possible white ones, such as snowdrops or even daisies.

+ Now take the initiative and take steps to move your life forward by going out socially where you may meet new people or to contact friends you may have avoided in your sorrow.

A Ger crossroads spell to avoid making the same mistakes again

Crossroads were traditionally believed to be places of power and because of this were used to bury illness and sorrows.

+ Take your Ger rune to a place where you can see cars, trains or boats passing.

+ As you hold it in your right hand (for left-brain intervention), choose a vehicle or boat and visualise yourself travelling on board – the destination is unimportant.

+ Feel the wind blowing your hair as you leave stagnation behind and see water cascading down in shimmering waterfalls.

+ Now take a short journey with your Ger rune, into the countryside if possible, and find a crossroads.

+ Facing west, the direction of the setting sun, which represents the direction of what is moving out of your life, draw a Ger rune in a dark colour on a black stone so that you can barely see it.

+ If there is soil close to the crossroads, bury your Ger stone, wrapped in dark fabric, facing west, saying:

Ger, Ger, let me tread this path no more.

+ Walk back from the crossroads, taking a different path, to symbolise that you have trodden a particular way for the last time. If possible, travel home by a different route or mode of transport.

+ If the crossroads is an urban one, dispose of your Ger stone in a biodegradable bag in a refuse bin, on the western track from the crossroads.

An Eoh spell to lay an unresolved grief to rest

You can use a yew or cypress tree or a tree associated with endings in your region or a wooden item made from yew or cypress. Carry out this spell at dusk or during the Dark of the Moon when we can no longer see the moon in the sky.

✛ Take a pottery dish of salt.

✛ Scatter a circle of salt clockwise around the tree and, using water in which rose petals have been soaked, sprinkle water over the salt circle. Leave sufficient room that you can walk within the circle.

✛ Light myrrh incense for endings and for healing, and complete the triple circle of power around the yew by walking round the tree clockwise, making a circle of smoke.

✛ Standing within the triple circle, with your back against the tree for strength, face west and, in the remaining salt in the dish, mark out the Eoh symbol with a fallen twig, saying:

Yew of endings, salt of life, end of sorrow, end of strife.

✛ Using a wooden or ceramic spoon, add water until the salt has dissolved, saying:

Eoh go, Eoh flow, flow away.

✛ Leave the circle and visualise it fading anti-clockwise.

✛ Tip away the water into the soil and purify the dish with a few drops of pine or lemon essential oil, to remove any lingering sorrow.

A Peorth spell to keep in touch with your true self

This spell is best carried out mid-morning on a clear day.

✣ Find a large spider's web to represent the web of Fate spun by the three Norns. If you can find one after rain so that the drops of water shine in the sunlight, that is best of all.

✣ In front of the web, arrange a pathway of small stones in a spiral, ending at a central point, to represent the path inwards to the true self.

✣ Holding your Peorth rune in your left hand for intuitive right-brain power, follow the pathway of stones and chant softly:

Peorth, Peorth, Peorth, guide me ever inwards to the centre
of truth until you reach the core.

✣ On the innermost stone in your mini-labyrinth, draw or carve a Peorth symbol.

✣ Create a more permanent spiral pathway in your garden by planting flowers or grasses on either side of your stone spiral. Walk it whenever you experience self-doubt. If you do not have a garden, create your labyrinth in miniature in a large plant pot, using stones or tiny glass nuggets to mark out the pathway.

✣ Keep your Peorth stone in the centre as a reminder that you should always remain true to yourself.

An Eohl ritual for developing your intuitive powers

+ Find a piece of fossilised wood on the shore. A stone with a natural hole, found on a beach or close to a river, is said to offer the ability to look forwards and backwards through time. Alternatively, buy a small piece of amber, if possible containing a leaf or insect. (Amber is fossilised tree resin that is millions of years old.)

+ On any one of these, draw or paint your Eohl symbol. This will fuse the wisdom of thousands of centuries to your own innate store of experience.

+ In the evening, during the period when the Moon begins to wane, a good time for psychic and divinatory processes, light five pure white candles in a horseshoe shape and place them on a high shelf or on top of a cupboard where you can see the light above you when you lie flat on a couch or bed.

+ Take your Eohl rune and place it just above your eyes in the centre of your brow, where it is believed the third eye or psychic insight resides, and say:

> *Eohl, Eohl bring to me,*
> *What it is I need to see.*

+ Place the Eohl symbol in your left hand, for right-brain intuition, and, lying on the bed or couch, focus on a point of light from the central candle. If you wish, you can ask a specific question or simply allow insights to come.

+ Travel in your mind's vision towards the light and let it expand round you.

+ See the light as a curtain parting and walk through it into another dimension.

+ Let visions and daydreams of the past or other existences flash through your mind's eye and do not try to analyse or understand them.

✦ When you are ready, move back through the curtain to the candlelight and into your conscious world again.

✦ Afterwards, record either in words or pictures any images, flashes of colour, scents and half-recalled phrases from your astral travelling.

If you repeat this over a period of days and sleep with your Eohl rune beneath your pillow, reciting 'Eohl' softly over and over again as a mantra, you will find that your dreams are full of rich images and you become tuned into your psychic abilities in the everyday world as well as during meditation or divination. You will also find your rune reading becomes far more focused and you may know answers to your own questions and those of others quite spontaneously through accessing this deeper well of wisdom.

A Sigil fire spell to get the job that you want

This spell is best carried out on the day of the Full Moon when her power is greatest, at noon so that you can harness both lunar and solar powers, representing the conscious and unconscious worlds. The summer solstice, or longest day, when the Sun is at its maximum power is best of all and if possible you should work outdoors in brilliant sunlight.

✦ Draw four Sigil runes on yellow crystals or yellow stones and place them in a circle in the centre of a golden disc of foil to represent the Sun.

✦ Position a rune at each of the four main compass points, beginning in the south, the direction of the Sun.

✦ Right in the centre of the foil, paint a large black dot. A circle with a dot in the centre is the astrological sign for the Sun.

✣ On the spot, place a lighted candle, which may be coloured red for energy, orange for self-assurance or gold for prosperity, inside the circle of crystals. They are all colours of the Sun. Use a broad candle holder and a small metal tray so that wax will not spill out.

✣ On a piece of red or orange paper, write a description of the job you want (it may be one you have seen advertised or a hypothetical one), including ideal location, salary and as many details as you can think of that would make it the perfect position. As you write, visualise yourself in a specific location or building, carrying out the work.

✣ When you have finished, consign the paper to the flame, all the while chanting softly:

Sigil, Sigil, Sigil, fill me with fire,
That I may gain what I desire,

until the paper has become ash and disappeared.

✣ Tip the ash on to white paper and, holding both ends of the paper, shake it gently until it forms a picture. If you cannot see one, close your eyes, blink and then open them. This will offer insight into the steps you should take for success.

✣ Leave your candle in a safe place and let its flame burn down naturally.

✣ When the wax has set, carve the Sigil sign in it and keep this on your window ledge until the week of the Last Quarter of the Moon.

Now take the first step towards getting your ideal job or career change: send for information, join a course that will make you better qualified or try the local job centre one more time. In the interim, tackle your present work with new enthusiasm so that you will get the promotion you desire and be ready to make the leap when a better offer comes your way. If you are unemployed, throw yourself into job-seeking with renewed vigour, considering new fields or areas further from your present home that may have relocation benefits attached.

Rune spells using the aett of Tir

A Tir wish spell

⁜ Wait until the stars are shining in the sky and take your Tir rune into the garden.

⁜ Using a star map, try to identify the Pole Star or choose the first star to shine in the evening sky.

⁜ Focus on it and visualise a ray of light coming from it and surrounding you in brightness.

⁜ Repeat what is probably the oldest magical spell in the world,

Star light, star bright, first star I see tonight,
I wish I may, I wish I might, have the wish I wish tonight.

⁜ Think very carefully before wishing and then, as you make your wish, turn over your Tir rune.

A Beorc spell for fertility

This is a spell best carried out when the Crescent Moon first appears in the sky. You should find a sheltered place where birch trees are growing; a grove of silver birch trees would be perfect (silver being the colour of the Moon) or paint branches silver if you are working indoors. You can substitute any fertility trees, for example an orchard of apple trees.

✣ Make nine bows of silver ribbon and attach them to a chosen tree or branch.

✣ Place your Beorc rune on top of something made of copper, the metal of Nerthus, the Earth Mother, and Frigga, the Norse Mother Goddess.

✣ Light mimosa incense, which is associated with Moon Mother energies, and circle your rune three times with the incense, making a triple circle of smoke.

✣ Whisper softly:

> *Beorc, Beorc, Beorc, Mother of the Earth, Moon Mother,*
> *I offer you my gifts, make my venture fertile.*

✣ Holding your Beorc rune in your left hand, turn your piece of copper over in your right hand for power, as you do with money at the New Moon and ask in your own words that as the Moon increases so will your fertility.

✣ When you return home, take a small tray of earth from the grove or garden and bury your copper object in it. Three days before the Full Moon, plant mimosa seedlings or another flower that is fragrant at night, such as night stock.

An Eh spell to restore your inner harmony

✤ Encircle yourself with small crystals of soft colours, if you have them, or glass nuggets of gentle hue.

✤ Draw an Eh rune and holding it in your power hand – the one you write with – think of each anxiety or resentment separately.

✤ Using silver or gold thread, make a small tangled skein for the first anxiety and place it in a glass jar; as you form each knot, tangle your resentment or whatever negative feelings you have in it.

✤ As you place the tangled negativity in the jar, say:

Eh, Eh, transform my anger/resentment/worry into a star.

✤ See it in your mind's eye, uncoiling and spiralling into the sky to form a star.

✤ Repeat the process for the second worry and continue tangling threads of negativity and consigning them to the sky until you feel calm.

✤ Place your Eh rune in the jar of threads and leave it open to the sunlight for a week. Then dispose of the threads and jar.

A Man spell to help with an important challenge

✤ Place your Man rune on a symbol of the challenge before you – a printer cartridge if you are submitting a thesis or a book to a publisher, a tool for a practical exam, a book for a course of study.

✛ Use a bright white stone or clear quartz crystal, pointed at one end like a magic wand, or attach a crystal point to a hazel rod, to make a traditional magic wand.

✛ Hold your symbol high in your left hand and direct the positive creative stone or crystal towards the sky in your power hand (the one you write with).

✛ See the light from your wand catching the light in the sky and trace a huge Man symbol in the light, saying:

> *Man, Man light my way to the success I need and the recognition I desire.*

✛ Draw a Man rune on a tall plank of wood or a broom handle and plant it in your garden, facing towards the place where you will take your exam – this is called a Nyd Pole and was placed outside Viking homes to attract power or repel negativity.

A Lagu spell for speaking the love in our hearts

✛ Draw a Lagu rune on a stone you found in flowing water and take it to the sea or to any tidal or fast-flowing river. If you are by the sea, wait until the tide is turning.

✛ Speak the words of love or longing either silently in your heart or softly into the wind and as you do so cast your symbol of emotion into the tide or the fastest point of the stream, saying:

> *Lagu, Lagu, carry my words to the heart of him or her to whom I call.*

✛ Now trace your Lagu symbol in the sand or soft earth on the banks and feel the love welling in your heart and flowing free.

✛ Watch the tide wash it away or gently push the soil into the river.

An Ing spell to relieve insomnia

+ Tie chamomile or lavender flowers into a net and run a bath so that the hot bath water flows over it. Alternatively, add a few drops of rose or chamomile essential oil to a full bath of water.

+ Light five soft pink candles on which you have carved Ing runes in the bathroom, then relax in your fragrant bath.

+ Afterwards carry your candles into the bedroom and, holding your Ing rune in your left hand, lie down and quietly chant:

Ing, Ing, quiet sleep,

as you see yourself floating gently through soft pink enveloping clouds.

+ See all your worries drifting away from the candle in tendrils of grey smoke, leaving you empty.

+ Do not try to create a vision or a scene or even to say any words, except for the protective mantra.

+ Blow out the candles, one by one, seeing the gentle light enveloping you and, as you close your eyes, let your vision be of a silver Ing at the head and foot of your bed, protecting you and bringing you a night of deep, dreamless sleep.

An Odal spell to find the right home

+ Place your Odal rune in the centre of a map of the area to which you wish to move. If you have no preferences or limitations, set the rune in the centre of a map of your country or even wider parameters if you suffer from wanderlust. Say:

Odal, Odal, far and wide,
Find a home where I may bide,
Across water, sky or near,
Show me the house I could hold dear.

✢ Place squared tracing paper over the map and, taking the Odal rune in your power hand, cast it from the south-east corner of the map.

✢ Cast your rune into the air, saying:

Odal, Odal, take me home,

and mark the spot it lands with a cross.

✢ Next, cast your Odal from the north-east corner of the map and again mark the spot it lands.

✢ Cast your Odal for a third time, this time from the central point of the bottom edge of the map.

✢ Draw straight lines from each of the three points across the map on the tracing paper and the point at which the lines intersect will provide your ideal location.

✢ Note the name of the town or village, or the grid reference, and using a more detailed map look for any identifying features: whether it is near a river, a wood or a shopping precinct. If there are street names, see if the chosen one has any significance for you.

✢ Even if the location seems an unlikely spot for you to live, consider it carefully and if possible visit the area before dismissing it. Seemingly random choices can reflect underlying needs and desires of which we are scarcely aware. Many a country dwelling commuter quit the city on an apparent impulse and never regretted it.

✢ Sleep for two or three nights with your Odal rune under your pillow and you may dream of your future home.

✢ As soon as you wake, write down any unusual features of the property and when you visit your chosen area, you may recognise it from your dreams.

A Daeg spell for bringing light to a gloomy room or house or working environment

+ Choose a sunny day when the light is at its most clear in your house or office, which can vary according to the way it faces.

+ Take a mirror and place it so that it reflects the light.

+ Paint a Daeg rune on a clear quartz crystal and hold it up to the mirror, saying:

*Daeg of light, Daeg of Dawn, shed your light upon this room.
Daeg of radiance, Daeg so bright, dispel gloom,
make day from night.*

+ Visualise the Daeg symbols multiplying as golden beams, reflecting off the mirror and filling the whole area with light.

+ Open the door of the workroom or the back door of the house to let out all the darkness and plant or place a vase of marigolds, golden carnations, chrysanthemums or any yellow flowers on either your desk or a table in the centre of the room to prevent darkness returning.

+ Leave the mirror in place throughout the sunlight hours.

+ In the evening at home or before you leave work, burn a golden or natural yellow beeswax candle and light frankincense or rosemary, incenses of the Sun.

+ Finally, paint and cut out a huge golden Daeg of foil and hang it in your window as a suncatcher, surrounded if you wish by yellow and clear quartz crystals on strings.

Rune spells using the aett of Odin

An Ac spell to resist emotional blackmail
or pressures to conform

+ Go to a forest or grove with oak trees and find a strong, fallen oak branch.

+ Carve a row of Ac symbols on one side.

+ As you etch each one, say:

   Ac stand strong, Ac stand true, as I ask power from you.

+ As you work, visualise each of your signs becoming a mighty oak growing around, protecting you.

+ Plant your Ac staff in your garden, facing towards the place where your emotional blackmailer lives.

+ If the person who is pressurising you is a member of your immediate family, place the stave horizontally beneath the foot of your bed or behind the door with the symbols facing outwards.

+ At the next difficult encounter, hold your Ac rune in your right hand for assertive energies; alternatively, make an Ac rune on wood or stone, drill a hole through it and wear it on a thong around your neck.

+ As you negotiate, visualise the oaks standing strong and do not bow to unfair pressure.

An Aesc spell to heal a polluted area or protect an endangered species of animal, bird or plant

✢ Visit a place where you can see the endangered species or carry out the spell while a video of the creatures is running on a day when rain is gently falling or it is misty.

✢ Wrap your Aesc rune in a grey or misty white cloth or scarf, saying:

> *Aesc, enfold in your branches all creatures who need protection. Keep them safe, keep them warm that they may heal, increase, re-grow within your sanctuary.*

✢ Bind the cloth with fronds of ash or any tree from your own region that shelters birds and animals within it.

✢ Enclose it in a small, old, wooden or tin box and after dark bury it in your garden or hide the box in a secret place and tell no one about its location.

A Yr spell to reach a new goal after failure

✢ If you can gain access to an archery range, place a paper Yr rune in the centre of a target. Aim your bow, focusing on your new goal.

✢ As you loose the arrow, call out:

> *Yr, Yr, make your mark.*

+ Alternatively, use a toy bow and arrow and target, or kick a football, on which you have painted an Yr symbol, towards a makeshift goal. Even an elastic band from which you flick an Yr symbol drawn on paper and screwed into a tight ball of energy will serve, as long as you physically direct your Yr power towards a specific target.

It does not matter if you do not hit the target. You can refine your aim in the actual situation once the energies are in motion.

An Iar spell for finding an alternative path

+ Go to a pathway that splits into two but ends up in the same place, albeit by different routes. Urban paths or mazes are a good source of such tracks, as are walkways on urban estates. If possible, find tracks surrounded by greenery.

+ Stop at the intersection and take the unfamiliar path or the one you least prefer, saying:

Iar, Iar, open new directions to channel my energies.

+ In your power hand (the one you write with), hold an Iar rune that you have etched on wood or stone.

+ As you walk along the unfamiliar pathway, use the other hand to scatter either tiny seeds or breadcrumbs that will be picked up by birds and so not litter the area; notice positive features and plan alternative steps you can take in your life if one path is blocked.

+ When you reach the destination, go back by the first path and leave your Iar rune in bushes or by the intersection, shedding with it any regrets or doubts.

An Ear spell to bring vitality back into your life

+ Take a dish of dry sand or dust and run your fingers through it, feeling its aridity and futility.

+ Fill a bottle or jar with the sand or dust and, as you tip each handful in, let your own exhaustion and depression trickle into the bottle, leaving you empty of emotion.

+ Put on the lid when the bottle or jar is full. Draw the rune Ear on the label to mark the contents as spent.

+ Go to a rich fertile field on a windy day and open your bottle, letting the dust blow away to fall on the fertile soil, saying:

Ear, Ear,
Scatter far,
Dead you are.

+ Fill the empty bottle with rich soil and take it to your garden or place the soil in a flower pot and plant a fast-growing seed, such as mustard and cress, so that before long, new life will return.

+ If you are careful you can sow your seeds to form the rune symbol Ear.

Further reading

Runes

Marijane Osborn and Stella Longland, *Rune Games*, Routledge and Kagan Paul, 1988.

Nigel Pennick, *Runic Astrology*, Aquarian Thorsons, 1990.

R.I. Pages, *Reading the Runes*, University of California Press, British Museum, 1996.

Paul Taylor and W.H. Auden, *The Elder Edda, Readings from the Icelandic*, Faber and Faber, 1983.

Edred Thorsson, *At the Well of Wyrd*, Samuel Weiser, Maine, 1988.

Edred Thorsson, *Futhark, A Handbook of Rune Magic*, Samuel Weiser, Maine, 1989.

Candles

Ray Buckland, *Advanced Candle Magick*, Llewellyn, 1997.

Ray Buckland, *Practical Candleburning Rituals*, Llewellyn, 1982.

Cassandra Eason, *Candle Power*, Blandford, 1999.

Herbalism, magic and incenses

Nicholas Culpeper, *Culpeper's Colour Herbal*, W. Foulsham & Co., 1983

Scott Cunningham, *Encyclopaedia of Herbs*, Llewellyn, 1997.

Scott Cunningham, *The Complete Book of Oils, Incense and Brews*, Llewellyn, 1993.

Cassandra Eason, *Every Woman a Witch*, W. Foulsham & Co., 1996.

You can visit Cassandra's website at
http://www.cassandraeason.co.uk

Index